DETAIL Practice

Energy-Efficiency Upgrades

Principles
Details
Examples

Clemens Richarz
Christina Schulz
Friedemann Zeitler

Birkhäuser Basel · Boston · Berlin

Edition Detail Munich

Authors:
Clemens Richarz, Prof. Dipl.-Ing. Architect, Energy Consultant
Munich University of Applied Sciences, Department of Architecture, Munich

Christina Schulz, Dipl.-Ing. Architect, Energy Consultant, Munich
Friedemann Zeitler, Dipl.-Ing. Architect, Energy Consultant, Building Adviser
Penzberg

Project manager:
Andrea Wiegelmann, Dipl.-Ing.

Editors:
Nicola Kollmann, Dipl.-Ing.(FH), Christina Schulz, Dipl.-Ing. Architect

Drawings:
Norbert Graeser, Silvia Hollmann, Claudia Hupfloher, Nicola Kollmann, Elisabeth Krammer,
Matthias Krupna, Andrea Saiko, Medin Verem

©2006 Institut für internationale Architektur-Dokumentation GmbH & Co. KG, Munich
An Edition DETAIL book

ISBN 978-3-7643-8121-9
Printed on acid-free paper made from cellulose bleached without the use of chlorine.

Typesetting & production:
Peter Gensmantel, Andrea Linke, Roswitha Siegler, Simone Soesters

Printed by:
Wesel-Kommunikation, Baden-Baden

1st edition 2007

This book is also available in a German language edition (ISBN 3-920034-14-7).

A CIP catalogue record for this book is available from the Library of Congress,
Washington D.C., USA.

Bibliographic information published by
Die Deutsche Bibliothek
Die Deutsche Bibliothek lists this publication in the Deutsche Nationalbibliographie; detailed
bibliographic data is available on the internet at http://dnb.ddb.de.

Institut für internationale
Architektur-Dokumentation GmbH & Co. KG
Sonnenstraße 17, D-80331 Munich
Tel.: +49/89/38 16 20-0
Fax: +49/89/39 86 70
www.detail.de

Distribution Partner:
Birkhäuser – Publishers for Architecture
PO Box 133, 4010 Basel, Switzerland
Tel.: +41 61 2050707
Fax: +41 61 2050792
e-mail: sales@birkhauser.ch
www.birkhauser.ch

DETAIL Practice
Energy-Efficiency Upgrades

Contents

Introduction

Clemens Richarz

Some 20% of the world's population consumes about 80% of the energy available worldwide. If we consider the growth forecasts for the newly industrialised countries, it becomes clear that we shall increasingly have to focus on reducing our consumption of energy.

The problem of the finite nature of our energy reserves, the subsequent upward price spiral and the fight to gain a share of dwindling resources represent only one side of the coin. The other side is the risk to our environment caused by the build-up of carbon dioxide (CO_2) in the Earth's atmosphere released through the burning of fossil fuels. In the highly industrialised countries the building sector – through the construction and operation of buildings – accounts for about 50% of total CO_2 emissions. In Germany, for example, 20% stems from the production and transportation of building materials, and 30% from heating, ventilation, cooling and lighting.

All aspects of construction will therefore be increasingly influenced by a sensible – and hence sustainable – approach to our use of the resources vital to life on this planet, based on long-term life cycles. Upgrading all components and installations affecting the use of energy in the existing building stock is of utmost importance. The long-term viability of these buildings requires that they be refurbished and upgraded taking into account energy-efficiency and energy-saving aspects.

1 Predicted supplies of fossil fuels based on consumption continuing at present levels (position as of 2004).
Source: Federal Institute for Geosciences and Natural Resources, www.bgr.bund.de
2 CO_2 reduction targets
The signatories to the Kyoto Protocol have agreed to reduce global CO_2 emissions by 5% by 2012, based on the 1990 level. Every country contributes a different amount to the agreed reduction. The diagram shows the reduction targets for European countries.
3 Housing units in Germany according to year of completion. A housing unit has an average living area of 89.4 m^2 (position as of August 2003).
Source: Federal Statistical Office, www.destatis.de

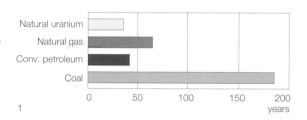

1

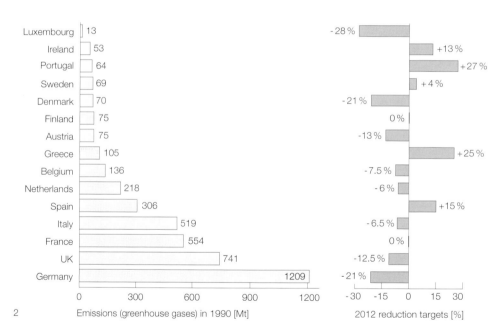

2 Emissions (greenhouse gases) in 1990 [Mt]   2012 reduction targets [%]

Housing units according to year of completion

Year	housing units	[%]
pre-1900	3 267 000	8.5
1901 to 1918	2 629 000	6.8
1919 to 1948	4 970 000	13.0
1949 to 1978	10 004 000	47.1
1979 to 1986	4 189 000	10.9
1987 to 2000	5 240 000	13.7
3 Total number of housing units	38 392 000	100

Development of regulations for the thermal performance of buildings with normal interior temperatures.

Date	Designation	Basis	Values
since 1952	Minimum thermal insulation	DIN 4108 (since Jul 1952) TGL 35424 (former GDR) currently: DIN 4108-2: (Jul 2003)	The aim is to avoid moisture damage through thermal insulation and to prevent overheating in summer. The following U-values may not be exceeded: wall 0.73 W/m²K roof to outside air 0.73 W/m²K floor to outside air 0.51 W/m²K floor to soil 0.93 W/m²K intermediate floor to unheated space 0.90 W/m²K
1 Nov 1977	1st Thermal Insulation Act	Energy Conservation Act 22 Jul 1976	*Thermal performance:* • $k_{m,max}$ depends on A/V (envelope area/heated vol.) ratio, (e.g. A/V = 0.8 → $k_{m,max}$ = 0.85 W/m²K) • $k_{m,AW+AF}$ < 1.85 W/m²K *Upgrade:* no requirements *Summer:* min. thermal performance to DIN 4108
1 Jan 1984	2nd Thermal Insulation Act	Energy Conservation Act	*Thermal performance:* • $k_{m,max}$ depends on A/V ratio, (e.g. A/V = 0.8 → $k_{m,max}$ = 0.66 W/m²K) • $k_{m,AW+AF}$ < 1.2 W/m²K • Joint permeability coefficient for windows limited to 1.0 m³/m h (daPa^{2/3}) *Upgrade (new):* • Component-based min. requirements for upgrades (wall 0.6 W/m²K; intermediate floor to outside air 0.45; floor over basement 0.7; double/insulating glazing for windows) *Summer:* • Min. thermal performance to DIN 4108
1 Jan 1995	3rd Thermal Insulation Act	Energy Conservation Act	*Thermal performance:* • Space heating requirement $(Q_T + Q_V - Q_s - Q_i)$ depends on A/V ratio *Upgrade:* • Component-based min. requirements for upgrades (wall 0.40 W/m²K; intermediate floor to outside air 0.30; floor over basement 0.5; windows 1.8) *Summer:* • Summertime thermal performance calculated as product of g_f and f, max. value 0.25
1 Feb 2002	Energy Conservation Act (revised 2004)	Energy Conservation Act (revised 10 Nov 2001) DIN standards	*Thermal performance:* • The specific transmission heat loss HT' related to the heat-transfer enclosing surface area is limited depending on A/V ratio. *Total balance (new):* • Primary energy requirement Q_p (heating and hot water) taking into account the plant is limited depending on A/V ratio. *Upgrade:* • Component-based min. requirements for upgrades (wall 0.35 W/m²K; intermediate floor to outside air 0.30 pitched/0.25 flat; floor over basement 0.4/0.5 new floor covering; windows 1.7); whole-building assessment possible as for new building (permissible values H_T' and Q_p'' may be exceeded by 40%). *Residential building/non-residential building (new):* • For the first time separate requirements for whole-building assessment (Q_p) *Summer:* • Calculation of s_{exist} and s_{max} and balancing of the two values.
2006 (proposed)	Energy Conservation Act	Energy Conservation Act (revised 8 Jul 2005 DIN standards (new DIN V 18599)	*Whole-building assessment (new):* • Compilation of total energy consumption (also ventilation, cooling, lighting) with max. values for H_T' and Q_p; separate methods for residential and non-residential buildings

4

Upgrades cut CO_2 emissions
As long ago as 1995, the preface to the German Thermal Insulation Act contained the following revelation: "The actual CO_2 reductions must be achieved in the existing building stock. The cross-ministry study group looking at this aspect assumes that a potential saving of about 100 million tonnes is possible, requiring an investment of some DM 350–400 billion (180–200 billion Euro)." It is therefore gradually becoming clear that CO_2 emissions due to the conditioning of building interiors can only be reduced by upgrading the vast majority of existing buildings (see figure 3).

Energy-saving legislation
When we look at developments in German legislation covering energy-saving aspects from the point of view of "measures in the existing building stock", the first detailed provisions can be found in the Thermal Insulation Act of 1984. Clause 8 of the Act specified minimum thermal insulation requirements for individual components which had to be observed when renewing facade, window and roof elements. The revised Act of 1995 retained the approach of its predecessor but with much more stringent maximum values.
Since the appearance of Germany's Energy Conservation Act in 2002 (updated in 2004), the plant and systems themselves, and hence the generation of the available heat required, has become an integral element of an energy efficiency evaluation. It is now no longer just the heating requirement that is considered, but also the primary energy input. This latter value includes all the energy-related output due to the generation of heat in the building itself plus the extraction and/or

production of the energy media employed (oil, gas, electricity, wood and other biomasses). The primary energy input is therefore also an indicator for the CO_2 output caused by heating a building. The new method valid for all buildings now permits an evaluation and estimate of measures for the existing building stock. For example, improvements to the passive thermal insulation can now be compared – in terms of their energy efficiency – with the replacement of an outdated boiler. For the first time, a comparison with a new building is also possible. However, besides the whole-building approach, the Energy Conservation Act also permits an assessment of individual values by means of component-related U-values, as has been known since 1984. The 2006 revision of the Act in the course of implementing the European Directive on "Energy Performance of Buildings" (2002/91/EC from 16 Dec 2002) will make the energy-related assessment more comprehensive and obviously much more complicated. Whereas the existing method will remain in place for residential buildings, all non-residential buildings will require the total primary energy input required for conditioning the building interior to be recorded and evaluated by means of defined target variables. Besides the energy required for heating, that required for lighting, for ventilation and for cooling will now have to be considered and grouped together in a primary energy parameter. The rules on which this is based are described in the draft standard DIN V 18599, which will form an intrinsic part of the revised Energy Conservation Act (see also pp. 97–105).

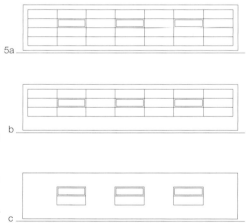

5a

b

c

5 The production energy for building components is calculated by taking the manufacturing energy values of the individual layers related to the lifetime of the layer (unit: kWh/a) and then adding these together. As so far there are no regulations (standards) for evaluating the production energy requirements that are binding for all building materials, the method is still not generally recognised. The diagram above shows three facade variations with respect to their embodied energy (surface area 50 m²). Calculations for this hypothetical assessment are based on heat-absorbing glass in wooden frames and the the non-glazed surfaces are calcium silicate masonry, thermal insulation, ventilated cavity and fibre-cement sheeting:
a fully glazed – 515 kWh/a – 185%
b partially glazed – 423 kWh/a – 152%
c totally closed – 278 kWh/a – 100%

Future developments
If we look to the future, or rather analyse the themes of the relevant research projects, it becomes clear that even this revision of the Act is not definitive for the energy-related assessment of building activities. For example, it is relatively easy – provided corresponding standardised and hence generally binding values are available – to determine the resources required for the production, maintenance and disposal of a building material (see figure 5). If data regarding the energy required to manufacture building products was included in tendering programs, it would be possible to calculate the use of resources for a building material, a building component or a whole building at the same time as preparing the tender documents, and this would then lead to optimisation.

Furthermore, it should be the aim of energy-related planning to consider not only the quantifiable use of resources for the construction of buildings and the conditioning of their interior climates, but also to understand these topics as part of the overriding theme of sustainability. Only then can we avoid treating energy issues in an isolated manner and, for example, presenting the thickness of the thermal insulation as the sole indicator of the energy performance assessment of a building.

Sustainable development of the building stock
The importance of a sustainable and energy-efficiency upgrade to a building can be illustrated by taking residential buildings as an example. Owing to their poor layouts, many apartments can only be let at huge discounts, regardless of whether their heating energy consumption already meets newer standards or not. As long as serious deficiencies, e.g. lack of contact with the outside world due to inadequate sizing or absence of balconies and windows, outdated sanitary facilities and, generally, insufficient floor space, cannot be eliminated, such apartments remain unappealing and hard to let. Experience shows us that this in turn leads to undesirable segregation processes in the demographics of the apartment block, the housing complex or even the whole district, with the associated potential for social conflict. Energy-efficiency upgrades to such apartment blocks that ignore the need to improve living standards on the whole do not fulfil the aims of sustainable, long-term, holistic approaches.

Besides improving the energy standards, sustainable refurbishment should involve changing the layouts to such an extent that they meet the needs of current and future tenants. Such work includes, for example, adapting bathrooms to the needs of older people or changing the interior layouts to achieve better flexibility of use (larger/smaller rooms, various user groups, etc.). We see the same problems in non-residential buildings. The conversion or further development of existing buildings generally involves not only energy aspects, but also always functional and architectural issues. The cooperation of the architect is therefore indispensable for sustainable refurbishment (see fig. 7).

Criteria for sustainable building

Society	• integration/assimilation • support for disadvantaged persons • participation
Urban planning	• urban identity • mix of living and work spaces • differentiated access (slow traffic!) • create prerequisites for using renewable energy sources
Natural resources/building land	• sealing of the surface • areas for traffic • integration into the landscape • protection of groundwater • use of rainwater
Building concept	• compactness • continued use of existing buildings • accessibility • flexible utilisation options • jointing of components (detachable, separable, reusable) • modular construction • production energy
Comfort	• lighting conditions • acoustic performance • thermal performance in summer and winter
Environmental and health compatibility	• low-emissions products (TVOC, CO, PCB) • low immissions through ionising and non-ionising radiation
Rational use of energy	• constructional measures (low space heating requirement, no overheating in summer) • plant measures (energy-efficient appliances, use of renewable energy sources)
Cost of usage	• cleaning • upkeep and maintenance • reduction in waste • water and waste-water ecology • separating components at the end of their useful life

6

Content of this book

As inadequate energy performance is frequently merely the starting point for further, more comprehensive refurbishment measures, the architect must possess some basic energy performance skills. Without knowledge in this area, it will in future be difficult to win corresponding commissions. The entire refurbishment process would probably be carried out without consulting an architect.

Architects with the necessary skills will be involved from the outset. In the course of the planning work, they can then illustrate the potential of a building as a whole and help ensure that energy performance measures are integrated into a viable, sustainable overall concept.

The intention of this book is to inspire the reader to incorporate energy-related themes into the design considerations for refurbishment measures, but also new building work. In order to create a direct reference to the statutory provisions, all energy performance issues are treated according to the objectives of the German Energy Conservation Act. In other words, the energy performance of a building is investigated for winter and summer conditions, and not just limited to residential buildings, but instead various types of building with their specific problems. Moreover, the plant technology is presented as an integral component of the overall energy performance concept.

The nature and extent of measures in existing buildings are frequently influenced by other conditions and regulations which concern the project management. Some examples of this are fire protection issues (fitness of components upon renewal), building law (altered clearances as a result of extensions and insulation measures), tax law (amortisation options for maintenance and construction costs, preservation orders for

monuments), building costs (subsidies, rent increases) and, above all, tenancy law (tenants' obligation to tolerate changes). The treatment of these topics would exceed the scope of this book. But as in any building project, such boundary conditions define the limits of feasibility and must therefore be clarified in advance.

We hope that this book will help the reader gain an insight into this topic, stir his interest and give him plenty to think about in terms of the sustainability issue as related to building refurbishment.

7a

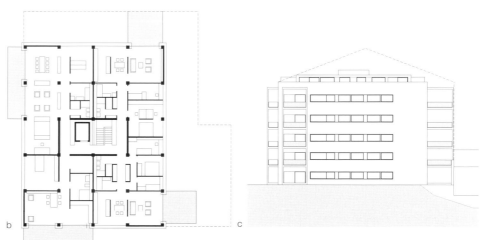

b   c

6 Sustainability criteria compiled from *Leitfaden nachhaltiges Bauen* (Guidelines For Sustainable Building), published by the Federal Ministry for Transport, Building and Urban Affairs, and Swiss standard SIA 112/1.

7 Conversion of the Sigl factory in Wasserburg
Conceptual study: Clemens Richarz
a existing building
b re-planned layout
c refurbished facade
The draft concept is based on converting an existing industrial building, which has stood empty for years, for residential use. The partial demolition of one longitudinal and one transverse grid line was, on the one hand, the prerequisite for obtaining approval by the building authorities and, on the

other, enabled the deep rooms of the former factory to be adapted for their new residential use. The existing concrete frame is ideal for converting into a "zero-energy house" with an accessible, adaptable plan layout. Aspects of the water and waste-water ecology are considered in the concept to the same extent as issues such as upkeep of the building in line with the useful life of the components. The parking spaces required can be incorporated in a new basement garage adjacent to the building without having to adapt the fabric of the building itself. The sustainable utilisation and refurbishment concept for this well-maintained but supposedly no longer usable industrial structure has had a positive impact on the entire district.

Principles

The quantity of energy required for conditioning building interiors depends on various parameters:

Interior climate
Human beings need a constant body temperature of 37°C. Creating a climate in which this body temperature can be maintained is therefore fundamental to human existence. The requirements for the conditioned space depend how that space is used, on the socio-cultural and economic boundary conditions.

Exterior climate
The amount of energy required to achieve the desired interior climate depends on the exterior climate, the constructional context and the expectations of the building's occupants.

Passive concept
In this approach the interior climate is essentially determined in relation to the exterior climate by means of the constructional concept. However, the expression "passive concept" indicates that the constructional measures merely react to the exterior climate and never actively influence the interior climate.
The form of the building plus the design of the building envelope and the load-bearing structure influence to a large extent the scope of the conditioning requirements. Constructional concepts that react to the climatic boundary conditions result in a much lower use of resources for conditioning than concepts that ignore this relationship.

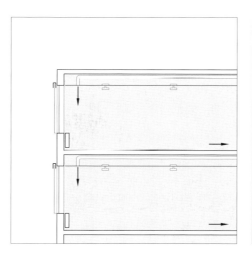

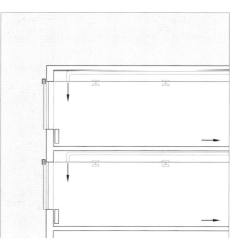

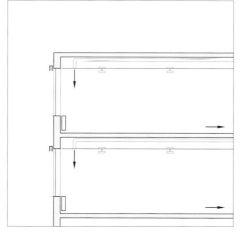

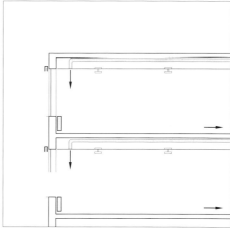

Active concept
The mechanical plant can be actively employed to influence the interior climate. The technical installation as a whole is therefore referred to as an active concept. The poorer the building's response to the prevailing climate and the greater the comfort demands of the occupants, the more comprehensive the technical installation will have to be – and will thus require more energy for its operation.

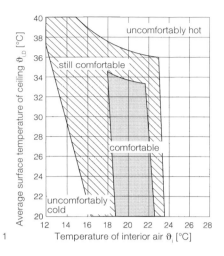

1   Temperature of interior air ϑ_i [°C]

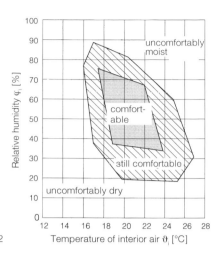

2   Temperature of interior air ϑ_i [°C]

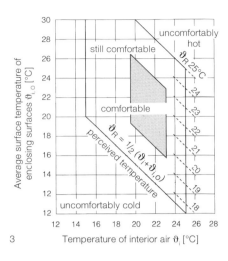

3   Temperature of interior air ϑ_i [°C]

Interior climate

The climate within a building should be such that comfortable, habitable conditions are created for the building's occupants or users.

Our feeling of comfort is influenced by physiological, psychological and hygienic factors. In an abstract sense, comfort is defined as the absence of disturbing factors.

Physical factors

The physical factors affecting comfort are easy to measure and assess, and can be broken down into the following parameters:

- temperature of interior air
- humidity of interior air
- temperature of enclosing surfaces
- movement of air near the body
- level of illumination
- use of daylight

The respective values are recorded separately but are always assessed with reference to each other (figures 1–3).

Hygiene factors

The hygiene boundary conditions are also quantifiable in the form of the quality of the air. To assess this, we measure the following parameters:

- CO_2 and oxygen content
- quantity of hazardous substances (formaldehyde etc.)
- concentration of micro-organisms (viruses, mites, spores)
- quantity of dust and particles
- olfactory quality (odours)

There is a direct relationship between air quality and air humidity. Humidity levels below 40% and above 60% offer good conditions for breeding micro-organisms. We therefore attach particular importance to maintaining a relative humidity of 40–60%.

Mould growth

Depending on the use of the building, an inadequate exchange of air generally leads to an increase in the interior humidity. This is almost always the case in older buildings when old, draughty windows are replaced by new types, but the ventilation habits of the users remain unaltered. Tightly sealed new windows reduce the "automatic" exchange of air that had been adequate in the past and this increases – initially unnoticed – the moisture content of the interior air. This situation becomes critical once the surface temperatures of the enclosing surfaces as a whole (due to insufficient thermal insulation) or locally (around thermal bridges) drop so low that the relative humidity rises locally to 80% or more. If this persists over several days for more than six hours a day, the growth of mould spores (which are always present in the air) is encouraged to such an extent that concentrations hazardous to health can build up.

Limit values for comfort in habitable rooms and ensuing requirements for external components

	Parameters influencing comfort		Season	Limit values		U-value [W/m²K]
1	Temperature of interior air	ϑ_i	winter summer	20 to 22 ≤ 26	°C °C	
2	Average temperature of enclosing surfaces	$\vartheta_{i,m}$	winter summer	≥ 17 ≤ 25	°C °C	≤ 1.25
3	Temperature difference between interior air (ϑ_i = 21°C) and component surface	$\Delta\vartheta$	winter	≤ 3	K	≤ 0.75
4	Temperature difference between opposite vertical components	$\Delta\vartheta$	winter	≤ 5	K K	≤ 1.25 (wall) ≤ 1.40 (window)
5	Temperature difference between floor and ceiling	$\Delta\vartheta$	winter	≤ 3	K	≤ 0.75
6	Temperature of floor surface	$\vartheta_{i,o}$	winter summer	17 to 26 ≤ 26	°C °C	≤ 1.25
7	Temperature of ceiling surface	$\vartheta_{i,o}$	winter summer	17 to 34 ≤ 34	°C °C	≤ 1.25
8	Heat flux density	q	winter	≤ 40	W/m²	≤ 1.25
9	Relative humidity of interior air	φ_i	winter summer	40 to 60 40 to 60	% %	
10	Relative humidity of interior air	V_L	winter summer	≤ 0.15 ≤ 0.30	m/s m/s	

1 Comfort range of human beings in enclosed rooms depending on temperature of interior air and ceiling
Applicability:
relative humidity 30–70%
movement of air 0–0.20 m/s
(after H. G. Wenzel and A. Müller)
2 Comfort range of human beings in enclosed rooms depending on temperature of interior air and relative humidity
Applicability:
average temperature of enclosing surfaces 19.5–23.0°C
movement of air 0–0.20 m/s
(after F. P. Leusden and H. Freymark)
3 Comfort range of human beings in enclosed rooms depending on temperature of interior air and average temperature of enclosing surfaces
Applicability:
relative humidity 30–70%
movement of air 0–0.20 m/s

temperature of all enclosing surfaces essentially equal
(after H. Reiher and W. Frank)
4 Water vapour content of the air for different temperatures and relative humidities. The grey boxes show examples of how ostensibly perfectly hygienic interior air conditions can still lead to mould growth problems local to thermal bridges even with a water vapour content of approx. 8.6 g/m³ (20°C, 50% r.h.) because at an air temperature of 12°C the critical limit moisture content of 80% is reached in the vicinity of these cooler surfaces.

The critical humidity level of 80% is reached even in normal interior conditions (50% relative humidity, 20°C air temperature) with a surface temperature of 12°C (see figure 4). Constructional thermal bridges (change of material in the facade) and geometrical thermal bridges (corners, reveals) are zones where this critical temperature can occur – by no means unusual in older buildings. This is illustrated by the isotherms of the simulations in the chapter entitled "Upgrading the construction".

It becomes clear that insulating the building envelope and eliminating thermal bridges not only decreases thermal losses, but also helps to reduce the probability of mould growth in the case of inadequate ventilation.

Assessing comfort
As in the past, the room temperature is still a key criterion for assessing comfort. Many standards (DIN 1946, 4108-2), statutory instruments (Energy Conservation Act) and directives (Places of Work Guidelines) specify 20°C as the lower and 26°C as the upper limit. Usable floor areas in buildings that cannot be heated to 20°C or which heat up beyond 26°C (which is frequently the case in summer) do not comply with codes of practice. This can lead to the users or owners claiming damages from the design team. The damages can be relatively accurately defined because it can be verified that human efficiency when performing non-manual activities drops considerably at temperatures below 20°C and above 26°C. These days, however, instead of just using rigid individual variables, comfort is being increasingly determined by way of a differentiated assessment, which takes into account type of activity and clothing as well as the aforementioned physical factors.

This method is described in DIN ISO 7730. The parameter here is called predicted mean vote (PMV), i.e. the anticipated average assessment of a certain interior climate by the room occupants. On a scale from -3 to +3, the comfort range lies between -0.5 and +0.5. The PMV value is correlated with the PPD (predicted percentage of dissatisfied) value.

Energy-efficiency upgrades
One aim of an energy-efficiency upgrade is to employ constructional and building services measures to eliminate disturbances to the feeling of comfort. Optimum upgrade concepts improve the feeling of comfort and at the same time reduce the use of energy for the conditioning of the building interior.

Water vapour content of the air for different temperatures and relative humidities

Air temperature [°C]	Water vapour content c [g/m³] for given relative humidity [%]									
	100	90	80	70	60	50	40	30	20	10
30	30.29	27.26	24.23	21.20	18.17	15.15	12.12	9.09	6.06	3.03
29	28.69	25.82	22.95	20.08	17.21	14.35	11.48	8.61	5.74	2.87
28	27.16	24.45	21.73	19.01	16.30	13.58	10.87	8.15	5.43	2.72
27	25.71	23.14	20.57	18.00	15.42	12.85	10.28	7.71	5.14	2.57
26	24.32	21.89	19.46	17.02	14.59	12.16	9.73	7.30	4.86	2.43
25	23.00	20.70	18.40	16.10	13.80	11.50	9.20	6.90	4.60	2.30
24	21.74	19.56	17.39	15.22	13.04	10.87	8.69	6.52	4.35	2.17
23	20.54	18.48	16.43	14.38	12.32	10.87	8.69	6.52	4.35	2.17
22	19.39	17.45	15.52	13.58	11.64	9.70	7.76	5.82	3.88	1.94
21	18.31	16.48	14.65	12.82	10.98	9.15	7.32	5.49	3.66	1.83
20	17.27	15.55	13.82	12.09	10.36	8.64	6.91	5.18	3.45	1.73
19	16.29	14.66	13.03	11.40	9.77	8.14	6.52	4.89	3.26	1.63
18	15.36	13.82	12.28	10.75	9.21	7.68	6.14	4.61	3.07	1.54
17	14.47	13.02	11.57	10.13	8.68	7.23	5.79	4.34	2.89	1.45
16	13.62	12.26	10.90	9.54	8.17	6.81	5.45	4.09	2.72	1.36
15	12.82	11.54	10.26	8.98	7.69	6.41	5.13	3.85	2.56	1.28
14	12.06	10.86	9.65	8.45	7.24	6.03	4.83	3.62	2.41	1.21
13	11.34	10.21	9.08	7.94	6.81	5.67	4.54	3.40	2.27	1.13
12	10.66	9.60	8.53	7.46	6.40	5.33	4.26	3.20	2.13	1.07
11	10.01	9.01	8.01	7.01	6.01	5.01	4.01	3.00	2.00	1.00
10	9.40	8.46	7.52	6.58	5.64	4.70	3.76	2.82	1.88	0.94
9	8.82	7.94	7.06	6.18	5.29	4.41	3.53	2.65	1.76	0.88
8	8.27	7.45	6.62	5.79	4.96	4.14	3.31	2.48	1.65	0.83
7	7.75	6.98	6.20	5.43	4.65	3.88	3.10	2.44	1.55	0.78
6	7.26	6.54	5.81	5.08	4.36	3.63	2.91	2.18	1.45	0.73
5	6.80	6.12	5.44	4.76	4.08	3.40	2.72	2.04	1.36	0.68

4

Climate zone A

Climate zone B

Climate zone C

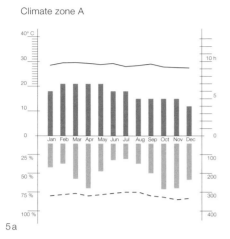

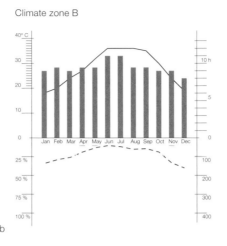

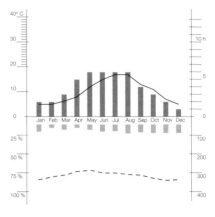

5a

b

c

Exterior climate

The temperature of the air, the length of exposure to solar radiation and the angle of incidence plus the amount of precipitation are dependent on the latitude and longitude of the site of the building. In particular, the amount of solar radiation – in conjunction with other geographical factors (ground surface characteristics, vegetation, bodies of water) – determines the exterior climate in which human beings have to survive.

Every climate zone or climate region has given rise to traditional building types which are a response to the respective climatic boundary conditions. Such buildings require – depending on the comfort requirements of their occupants – little or no mechanical services to ensure an agreeable climate in the habitable rooms.

Description of the climate
Table 6 after W. Koppen offers a model for an exact description of the characteristic climate of a region. The model classifies the prevailing regional conditions with the help of a graduated catalogue of criteria (climate zones, climate types, climate subtypes).
Taking the city of Würzburg in southern Germany as an example (which is used by the Energy Conservation Act as the reference location for the average climate in Germany), we can illustrate the method and its usefulness for planning optimised energy concepts:
· climate zone C
· climate type f
· climate subtype b
The climate situation in Würzburg is therefore designated as Cfb, which in layman's terms means a moist temperate climate with warm summers.
A building envelope with high standard of thermal insulation, a moderate window surface area of 20–50% and heat-storage elements in the interior (e.g. unclad solid

components) can react optimally to these climatic conditions. Only a comparatively low energy requirement is then necessary to create an agreeable climate in the habitable rooms. Even if the building is used for offices, these conditions will not require any air-conditioning systems for cooling in the summer, provided the proportion of windows is not increased and effective sunshades are available.

Energy-efficiency upgrades
In the event of an energy-efficiency upgrade, specific measures can be used to activate or re-activate natural, self-regulatory processes in the building. Examples of this are the improvement of the thermal behaviour by exposing storage masses, or the promotion of natural ventilation by creating cross-ventilation opportunities.

5a–f The diagrams show the monthly average values for climate zones A to E and the German reference climate (Würzburg) for the following parameters:
· outside temperature (———)
· relative humidity (– – – –)
· hours of sunshine (dark grey)
· precipitation (light grey)

6a–c Climate classifications after W. Köppen
a   Climate zones
A   Tropical rainforest or savannah climate without winter
The average temperature remains above 18°C every month.
B   Dry climate
Precipitation remains below a dry limit dependent on temperature and distribution of precipitation. If
r = annual total of precipitation [cm], and
t = annual average of temperature [°C],
the dry limit (limit value of r) is calculated as follows:
· for prevailing
winter rain $r = 2t$
· for even distribution of
precipitation $r = 2(t + 7)$
· for prevailing
summer rain $r = 2(t + 14)$
C   Warm temperate climate
The temperature of the coldest month lies between +18°C and -3°C; the total precipitation lies above the aforementioned dry limit.
D   Boreal forest climate
The temperature of the coldest month lies below -3°C; the temperature of the hottest month remains above +10°C.
E   Snow climate
The average temperature of the hottest month lies below +10°C.

b   Climate types
The letters that designate the climate types are defined below:
F   Permafrost climate
All the average monthly temperatures lie below 0°C.
T   Tundra climate
The average temperature climbs above 0°C for at least one month in the year.
S   Steppe climate
A dry region in which the amount of precipitation permits regular vegetation. Precipitation remains above a dry limit dependent on temperature and distribution of precipitation in order to distinguish between steppe and desert. When
r = annual total of precipitation [cm], and
t = annual average of temperature [°C],
the dry limit (limit value of r) is calculated as follows:
· for prevailing
winter rain $r = t$
· for even distribution
of precipitation $r = t + 7$
· for prevailing
summer rain $r = t + 14$

Climate zone D

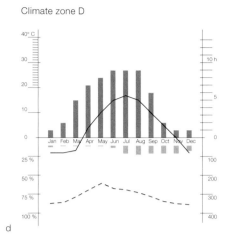

d

Climate zone E

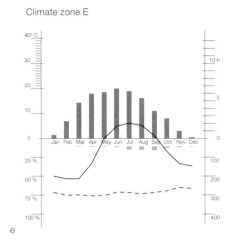

e

Germany (Würzburg)

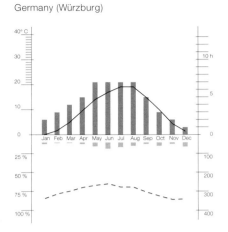

f

Climate zones

The climate zones are distinguished by five capital letters:

	Code letter	Description	Example
1	A	Tropical rainforest or savannah climate without winter	Malaysia
2	B	Dry climate	Saudi Arabia
3	C	Warm temperate climate	Great Britain
4	D	Boreal forest climate	Finland
5	E	Snow climate	Greenland

6a

Climate zones

A second letter is added to distinguish between 11 climate types:

	Code letter	Description	Example
1	Af	Tropical rainforest climate	Kuala Lumpur
2	Aw	Savannah climate	Bombay
3	BS	Steppe climate	Alicante
4	BW	Desert climate	Kuwait
5	Cw	Warm, dry-winter climate	Lhasa
6	Cs	Warm, dry-summer climate	Rome
7	Cf	Moist temperate climate	Stuttgart
8	Dw	Dry, cold winter climate	Beijing
9	Df	Dry, moist winter climate	Moscow
10	ET	Tundra climate	Svalbard, Spitsbergen
11	EF	Permafrost climate	Mirny, Antarctica

b

Climate subtypes

Another letter can be added to the climate type to make further distinctions:

	Code	Description	Example
1	a	Hot summer	Marseille
2	b	Warm summer	Karlsruhe
3	c	Cool summer	Reykjavik
4	d	Severe winter	Verhojansk
5	g	Ganges-type annual temperature progression	New Delhi
6	h	Hot	Karachi
7	k	Cold	Teheran

c

W Desert climate
  Dry climate in regions with very little or no precipitation. The precipitation remains below the
  aforementioned dry limit.
f Moist
  All the months are wet; the quantity of precipitation in the driest month in the A climate is at
  least 60 mm.
m Hybrid form, rainforest climate despite a dry
  period
  In the Am climate, the precipitation remains below 60 mm in one or more months. The lack of
  precipitation is made up for in the other months
  so that the tropical rainforest remains intact.
  The quantity of precipitation in the driest month
  is more than 4% of the difference 2500 mm –
  annual precipitation. Example: Yangon

Driest month [mm]						
60	50	40	30	20	10	0
Annual precipitation at least [mm]						
1000	1250	1500	1750	2000	2250	2500

s Dry summer, dry period during summer of
  hemisphere concerned
  The driest summer month has less than 40 mm
  and less than 1/3 of the total precipitation of the
  wettest winter month.
w Dry winter, dry period during winter of hemisphere concerned
  The average precipitation of the driest winter
  month is less than 1/10 of the precipitation of
  the wettest summer month. In the A climate the
  driest month has less than 60 mm and less
  than the dry limit for the Am climate.

c Climate subtypes
a Hot summer
  Average temperature of hottest month higher
  than +22°C.
b Warm summer
  Average temperature of hottest month below
  +22°C; at least four months with an average
  temperature of at least +10°C.
c Cool summer
  Average temperature of hottest month below
  +22°C; up to three months with an average
  temperature of at least +10°C.
d Severe winter
  Average temperature of coldest month below
  38°C.
g Ganges-type annual temperature progression
  The annual maximum occurs before the summer solstice and the summer rainy season.
h Hot
  Average annual temperature higher than
  +18°C.
k Cold
  Average annual temperature below +18°C.

Source: Heyer: Witterung und Klima,
B. G. Teubner Verlagsgesellschaft, Stuttgart, 1988

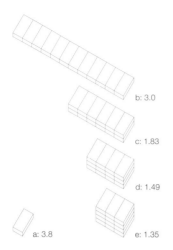

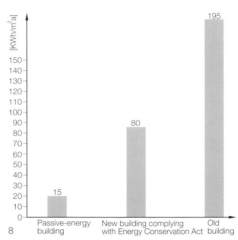

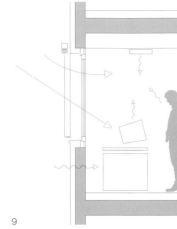

7   a: 3.8   e: 1.35   8   9

Passive concept

The constructional concept of the building can help to influence the following parameters:
- heat losses in winter
- overheating in summer
- natural ventilation options
- scope for daylight utilisation

The interior temperatures fluctuate to different extents depending on the form of the building itself (compactness), the design of the envelope (building materials, orientation, amount of glazing), the loadbearing structure (heavyweight, lightweight) and the exterior climate. If interior temperatures do not achieve a defined standard of comfort, building users experience a less-than-agreeable interior climate.

Such deficits must then be overcome by the mechanical plant if optimisation of the building itself is no longer possible.

Heating requirement

The heating requirement describes the quantity of heat that must be supplied to a room in order to achieve and maintain the desired room temperature. The heating requirement is made up of the following factors:
- heat losses through transmission
- heat losses through ventilation
- heat gains through incident solar radiation
- heat gains through the use of the room (persons, equipment)

The heating requirement is therefore dependent on the thermal transmittance (U-value) of the building envelope, the size and orientation of windows, the quantity of external air that enters the building uncontrolled and the quantity of heat generated by heat sources in the room itself.

Cooling requirement

Irrespective of any building services, the following heat sources can cause a room to heat up:
- incident solar radiation
- incoming warm external air
- transmission
- use of the building

The quantity of cold air that must be fed into a room to prevent overheating is known as the cooling requirement.

The cooling requirement of a building depends on the size, orientation and design of the window areas (sunshades, type of glazing), the availability of storage mass and the natural ventilation options. Natural ventilation in conjunction with storage mass are particularly important because heavyweight building components can absorb a large quantity of heat without undergoing a significant temperature increase. Cool night-time air can help the stored heat to escape again – at least partially.

---

7   The compactness, defined as the ratio of the envelope surface area to the net area on plan, is the principal feature of a draft concept optimised for energy performance. The diagram shows a basic module (a) measuring 20 × 10 × 3.5 m which has a conditioned usable floor space of 160 m². The usable floor space can be organised into different compact building types (b-e). If, for example, the usable floor area is accommodated in a three-storey volume instead of a row, the area of the envelope is reduced by half. Increasing the compactness (while maintaining the same standard of building) reduces the energy requirement considerably.

8   The heating requirement of an older building is approx. 200 kWh/m². The lion's share of this results from the high transmission heat losses through the poorly insulated envelope surfaces. The use of constructional measures and a ventilation system with heat recovery can bring down the heating requirement to as little as 15 kWh/m²a. Buildings with such a low heating requirement are known as "passive-energy buildings". Buildings with a thermal insulation and installation standard in accordance with the Energy Conservation Act (new buildings) have a heating requirement of approx. 80 kWh/m²a.

9   If external loads (solar radiation, ventilation, transmission) and internal loads (persons, machines, lighting) cause interior temperatures to rise above the comfort limit, the excess heat must be purged: a cooling requirement ensues.

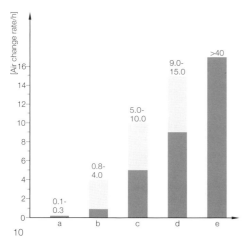

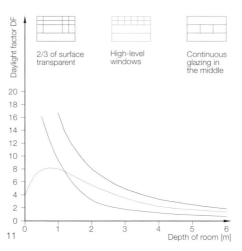

Ventilation

The energy requirement for supplying fresh air to a building depends on whether and to what extent the building can be ventilated naturally. The quantity of air required for hygienic conditions can be determined either with respect to the number of occupants or to the net volume of the room. The per person requirement is on average 30 m³/h. The quantity of fresh air that must be supplied (per hour) to habitable rooms in relation to their net volume is known as the air change rate; according to DIN 4108-2 it must be at least 0.5. It is frequently forgotten that ventilation problems are due not only to too much air being exchanged (which results in an increased heating or cooling requirement and hence worsens the energy balance). Problems can also ensue from an inadequate exchange of air, which means that hygienic air conditions are impossible (see p. 14). As the natural ventilation options are heavily dependent on the habits of the building's occupants as well as the type of building itself, the air change rate can only be controlled precisely with some form of mechanical backup. Designers are therefore recommended to include a ventilation system ("controlled ventilation" with or without heat recovery) in naturally ventilated buildings.

Lighting

The amount of energy required for illuminating the interior of a building depends on the quantity of daylight available and users' requirements regarding brightness, contrast and distribution of light within the interior.

The size, arrangement and quality of the windows (the glass), the degree to which they are shaded plus the depth of the room to be illuminated and the reflective capacity of its surfaces determine the proportion of daylight that can be used for lighting the interior. The daylight factor (DF) describes the ratio of the level of illuminance on a work surface in a room to the level of illuminance in the open air with an overcast sky. This factor is ideal for describing the quality of the daylight at a certain workplace. An external level of illuminance of 10 000 lx and a daylight factor of 5% means that at the place under consideration in the room the level of illuminance is still 500 lx. DIN 5034 "Daylight in interiors" calls for a daylight factor of at least 0.75–1% at half the depth of the room, which means a level of illumination of 100 lx at that point. The upshot of this is that in order to achieve the level of illuminance necessary for workplaces (500 lx), artificial lighting must be switched on to make up the deficit of 400 lx.

Energy-efficiency upgrades

An energy-efficient upgrade may involve improving the constructional standard of any type of existing building.

Possible constructional measures include improving the thermal insulation, renewing the windows, eliminating thermal bridges, decreasing the solar heat gains by providing sunshades, or retrofitting of storage mass in the form of latent storage media. The natural ventilation behaviour of the building can be improved by installing weatherproof and intruder-proof window openings, and can be controlled precisely by installing a mechanical backup (e.g. extractor fan). Additional air ducts or atria can optimise the cross-ventilation of the building.

The proportion of daylight in the interior can be increased by a combination of larger windows and daylight optimisation measures. In non-residential buildings in particular, the aim should be to get an even spread of daylight as far into the building as possible.

However, please note that large areas of glazing increase the thermal loads in the summer and the sunshades required to combat this can lessen the amount of daylight entering.

10 The diagram shows the air change rates possible with natural ventilation:
   a doors and windows closed
   b windows tilted (minimal ventilaton cross-section)
   c windows half open
   d windows fully open
   e cross-ventilation
   The air change rate is either too high or too low with natural ventilation. An optimum air change rate of 0.5/h (50% of the volume of air is replaced by outside air every hour) is nearly impossible to obtain, even when occupants are aware of the need for proper ventilation. Precise control of the supply of outside air is only feasible with the help of a mechanical system.

11 Daylight factor in the interior for various window forms.
   The following principles should be considered when optimising the use of daylight:
   • top of window = underside of ceiling
   • continuous glazing instead of individual windows
   • opaque spandrel panels because glazing at floor level does not improve the amount of daylight further away from the windows, but instead merely increases the thermal loads

Active concept

Irrespective of the constructional concept, technical installations can be used to help achieve the desired interior climate – with a corresponding use of energy and resources, of course. However, it is advisable, from both the ecological and economic viewpoints, to employ constructional measures in the first instance to minimise the energy required to create comfortable internal conditions. The lacking energy should then be provided with efficient technologies which employ renewable energy sources.

Installations can be divided into the following main groups:
• heating
• cooling
• ventilation
• humidification and dehumidification
• lighting
In each type of installation we break down the components required into those for generating, storing, distributing and supplying the energy to the room.

Efficient installations
A building services installation is efficient when the losses during energy generation, distribution, storage and supply are kept to a minimum, and thus the quantity of energy contained in the raw material is exploited as fully as possible.
In all electrically operated equipment the energy required must be multiplied by the primary energy input in order to be able to compare it with other sources of energy in terms of the application of raw materials. A factor of 3 (value for Germany), for example, indicates that the generation of one kilowatt-hour of electricity consumes on average three kilowatt-hours of the quantity of energy contained in a fossil fuel (oil, coal, gas). In countries with a higher proportion of energy from nuclear power stations or renewable sources, the value is correspondingly lower (see also pp. 56–63).

Installations or active concepts are particularly economical when one appliance can fulfil several requirements. For example, a heat pump can be used for heating and cooling. Likewise, with the help of an absorption refrigerator, the heat from conventional boilers or district heating systems can be used for cooling as well. Appliances that generate electricity and heat simultaneously from one energy source are also frequently used. Such combined heat and power (CHP) systems

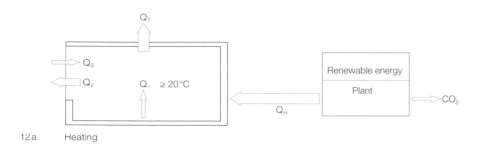

12a   Heating

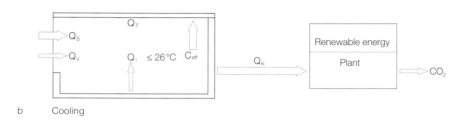

b   Cooling

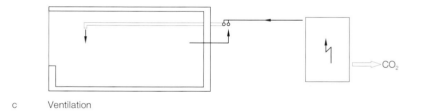

c   Ventilation

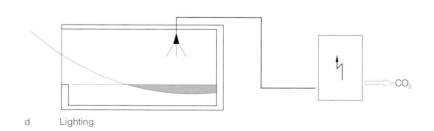

d   Lighting

12a The heating requirement in winter necessary to maintain comfortable conditions in the interior is generated by mechanical plant and fed into the rooms. The higher the proportion of renewable energy involved in this, the lower the CO_2 emissions.
b In order to achieve a comfortable interior climate during the summer, with the assistance of the mechanical plant sufficient heat must be removed from the rooms to ensure that the room temperature is not above, or only minimally exceeds, 26°C.

c In order to be able to ventilate a room sufficiently, it is advisable to use a mechanical ventilation system with a controlled air change rate. The energy required to operate the system (electricity for fans) must be taken into account in the energy assessment.
d The artificial lighting required to create adequate levels of illumination depends on the amount of daylight available inside the building. The quantity of energy required to operate the lighting must be taken into account in the energy assessment.

can be realised with small co-generation plants and fuel cells. However, CHP is only advisable for covering long-term, constant, basic loads and should be combined with another heating system in order to deal with peak loads. Ideal for this are, for example, gas-fired condensing boilers, which can react flexibly to different load requirements.

The efficiency of installations decreases, however, if they are operated in the heating period only, or even if they are operated the whole year round but the heat cannot be used in summer. When CHP is specified, it is therefore desirable to adopt a method of operation in which heat and electricity are generated and used continuously. One sensible use would be hot water provision, for example, although in this case a small co-generation plant would have to supply a larger number of buildings in order to obtain a useful amount electricity while generating heat. Storing the heat in a seasonal storage medium or running a refrigeration plant operated by heat are possible hybrid solutions which could do justice to the aforementioned aims.

Renewable energy
Installations that use renewable energy sources are very important. These are:
- solar collectors for generating heat
- photovoltaic cells for generating electricity
- air collectors for heating the air
- heat pumps for exploiting geothermal heat or groundwater
- ventilation systems for exploiting geothermal heat
- extract systems to achieve efficient night-time cooling

Heat from the ground (geothermal heat) is ideal for heating and cooling purposes because the temperature in the ground down to a depth of 80 m remains constant at 10–14°C. Using geothermal heat and a heat pump for heating purposes is especially effective, i.e. can be run with a high degree of efficiency with respect to the electricity input, when the building itself has only a low heating requirement. The resulting low flow temperatures in winter are exploited to the full by the heat pump.

Geothermal heating systems that can be used for heating and cooling are particularly efficient because the subsoil from which heat is extracted can be reheated in summer by the heat extracted from the building.

Innovative concepts
The development of systems now includes appliances and installations that use renewable energy sources with minimal primary energy input to achieve the desired internal conditions, e.g. heat pumps with an energy input of 1 kWh of electricity for extracting 4–6 kWh of warm or cool air from the environment (groundwater, soil). The primary energy input of 3 kWh associated with the use of electricity is thus more than made up for.

Even more efficient are gas-fired absorption heat pumps. And energy can be generated with hydrogen without using any resources. In this electrolytic process water is split into its constituent parts hydrogen and oxygen. The electricity required for this can be obtained via photovoltaic cells. The hydrogen stored in tanks can be burned directly to generate heat or can react with oxygen in a fuel cell. In this latter process electricity and heat are generated, and the final product is water again. However, such systems are still inefficient. About 97% of the solar energy incident on a photovoltaic panel is lost during the conversion process.

Energy-efficiency upgrades
In an energy-efficiency upgrade, renewal of the installations and the use of renewable energy sources can achieve a significant reduction in the consumption of energy and, above all, resources. Often, renewing the installations is the sole and, first and foremost, most effective way of achieving an energy-efficiency upgrade. If, for example, in an old building with an annual heating-oil consumption of 10 000 l, the old boiler with a degree of efficiency of 80% is replaced by a new boiler with a degree of efficiency of 95%, the annual oil consumption is reduced by about 1500 l. The greatest energy-savings are achieved when constructional and plant measures are combined and coordinated.

For example, improving the thermal insulation leads to a reduced heating requirement, which in turn can be handled by a much lower flow temperature. Such constructional measures are essential prerequisites for efficient installations using heat pumps, for instance. The combination of a gas-fired condensing boiler backed up by solar-powered heating is only really sensible when the building can be heated with a low flow temperature. Only under such conditions is optimum exploitation of the fuel and the solar energy possible.

Therefore, sustainable energy concepts must...
- determine whether the users' expectations are practicable,
- take account of the local climatic boundary conditions,
- reduce the energy requirement through constructional measures,
- optimise the final energy requirement through efficient installations, and
- minimise the primary energy input by selecting suitable energy sources.

Upgrading the construction
Building A

Taking a hypothetical residential building built sometime between 1950 and 1965 as our example, we shall demonstrate various energy-efficiency upgrade measures in terms of their constructional details and energy performance benefits. They will be presented as individual measures without being integrated into an overall concept. In other words, to take account of a large number of constructional circumstances in the existing building stock, the original situation will be redefined again and again for some measures. For example, in order to coherently illustrate certain upgrading measures, the building will be assumed to have reinforced concrete floors too, and not timber joist floors. The same is true for the roof covering, the windows and the render, the quality of which is assumed to vary in some instances. All the detail drawings have been drawn to a uniform scale of 1:10.

Our hypothetical residential building is a detached, two-storey, typical German suburban structure whose roof space has been converted into living accommodation, although a small unheated attic remains. The building contains three separate apartments which are accessed via a common staircase. The apartment in the roof space has low-level walls (with accessible eaves storage spaces behind) and sloping ceilings along the longitudinal sides. The basement is not classed as habitable space and is unheated. The central oil-fired heating and hot-water systems are located here, as are the oil tanks.

Since being built, the building has only undergone minor, cosmetic repairs. The one major investment was the installation of a new heating system in the basement in 1980. As the building is in need of refurbishment and the cost of energy is constantly on the increase, an energy-efficiency upgrade is to be considered.

Existing situation

A survey of the actual situation is one of the greatest challenges facing the designer because it will be used as the basis for assessing the energy-saving potential of various insulation and refurbishment measures. In many cases it is impossible to establish the exact nature of components such as walls or intermediate floors without using destructive inspection techniques. Avoiding these requires experience, intuition and an understanding of construction methods. The following provide invaluable help in such circumstances:

- original drawings
- building authority records
- invoices from contractors and tradesmen
- the DIN standards valid at the time of construction (information about building materials and forms of construction typical at that time)

During its field trials to establish a practical energy certificate, the German Energy Agency produced a table of thermal transmittance values typical for certain periods (figure 1). The energy consultants involved in the work were allowed to use the global U-values from the table or to calculate the U-values of the respective components individually.

The standard values according to the table have been used in our building A example. The reason: on the one hand, the inaccuracies in establishing the as-built construction of the existing building fabric are better covered by the global figures and, on the other hand, this approach is not influenced quite so much by regional differences in the workmanship. The following U-values have been taken from the table for Building A:

Typical U-values [W/m²K] for components in the building stock

	External wall			Topmost floor/ Flat roof			Pitched roof			Floor over basement/ Ground floor finishes		
Pre-1918	Clay bricks or coursed random rubblemasonry	E M	2.2*	Timber joist floor with straw loam infill	E M	1.0	No insulation, plaster on reed mats or lathing	E M	2.6*	Timber joist floor with straw loam infill	E M	1.0
	Timber frame with loam infill panels	E M	2.0*				Straw loam infill between rafters, plaster to underside	E M	1.3*	Stone floor on soil or vaulted basement	E M	2.9*
1880–1948	Clay brickwork, 250-380 mm	E M H	1.7*	Timber joist floor with subfloor and loam infill	E M	0.8	No insulation, plaster on reed mats or lathing	E M	2.6*	Timber joist floor with subfloor and loam infill	E M	0.8
	Single-leaf masonry, 380-510 mm, or double-leaf	E M	1.4*				Straw loam infill between rafters, plaster to underside	E M	1.3*	Solid brick-arch floor	E H	1.2
1949–1968	Lightweight masonry of hollow blocks, perforated bricks, aerated concrete	E M	1.4*	Concrete slab, ribbed slab, hollow-block floor	E M H	2.1*	35 mm wood-wool slabs, plastered	E M	1.4*	Concrete slab, ribbed slab, hollow-block floor with min. impact sound insulation	E M H	1.5*
	Masonry of solid pumice concrete bricks	E M	0.9	Timber joist floor with subfloor	E M	0.8	Solid pumice concrete bricks between rafters	E M	1.4*	Timber joist floor with subfloor	E M	0.8
							50 mm insulation between rafters	E M H	0.8			
1969–1978	Lightweight perforated clay bricks with normal-weight mortar	E M	1.0	Concrete slab with 50 mm topside insulation	E M H	0.6	35 mm wood-wool slabs, plastered	E M	1.4*	Concrete slab with 20 mm impact sound insulation	E M H	1.0
	Precast concrete elements with core insulation or of ltw. concrete	M H	1.1	Flat roof: concrete slab with 60 mm topside insulation (cold deck)	E M H	0.5	Solid pumice concrete bricks between rafters	E M	1.4*			
	Timber stud walls with 60 mm insulation	E	0.6	Timber joist floor with 40 mm insulation (timber structure/ turnkey house)	E	0.8	50 mm insulation between rafters	E M H	0.8			
1979–1983	Lightweight/vertically perforated clay bricks with lightweight mortar	E M	0.8	Concrete slab with 80 mm topside insulation	E M	0.5	80 mm insulation between rafters	E M	0.5	Concrete slab with 40 mm impact sound insulation	E M H	0.8
	Masonry of aerated concrete	E M	0.6	Flat roof: concrete slab with 80 mm insulation (warm deck)	M H	0.5						
	Precast concrete elements with core insulation, or of ltwt. concrete	M H	0.9	Timber joist floor with 80 mm insulation (timber structure/ turnkey house)	E	0.5						
	Timber stud walls with 80 mm insulation	E	0.5									
1984–1994	Lightweight/vertically perforated clay bricks with lightweight mortar	E M	0.6	Concrete slab with 120 mm topside insulation	E M H	0.3	120 mm insulation between rafters	E M H	0.4	Concrete slab with 50 mm impact sound insulation	E M H	0.6
	Masonry of aerated concrete	E	0.5	Timber joist floor with 120 mm topside insulation (timber/ structure turnkey house)	E	0.3						

E = detached house, M = apartment block, H = large apartment block/high-rise block

Source: dena (German Energy Agency)

1 * A global U-value of 1.0 W/m²K can be assumed for retrofitted insulating boards at least 20 mm thick.

1 Overview of the German building stock
2 Heat losses and gains of existing building in
   kWh/a. The savings due to night-time reductions
   are considered in the plant losses.

- external wall   1.4 W/m²K
- windows   2.8 W/m²K
- pitched roof surface   1.4 W/m²K
- spaces within eaves   1.4 W/m²K
- attic floor   0.8 W/m²K
- floor over basement   1.5 W/m²K

These assumptions result in an annual heating requirement of approx. 200 kWh/m²a. For simplicity, the entire heating installation is assumed to have a degree of efficiency of approx. 70%, which translates into an annual heating oil consumption of approx. 29 l/m² of heated usable space. Hot-water provision has been ignored in this calculation. If the individual measures proposed on the following pages were to be combined and the existing insulation retained, the annual heating oil requirement could be cut to less than 10 l/m².

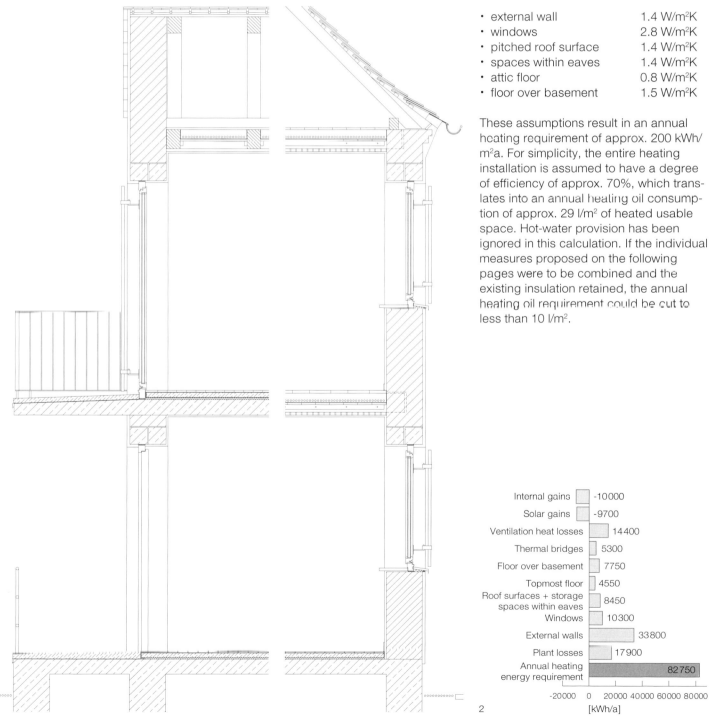

	kWh/a
Internal gains	-10000
Solar gains	-9700
Ventilation heat losses	14400
Thermal bridges	5300
Floor over basement	7750
Topmost floor	4550
Roof surfaces + storage spaces within eaves	8450
Windows	10300
External walls	33800
Plant losses	17900
Annual heating energy requirement	82750

-20000 0 20000 40000 60000 80000
[kWh/a]

2

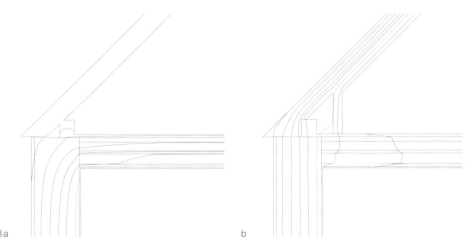

3a   b

Requirements to be satisfied by a pitched roof after upgrading:

max. U-value: 0.30 W/m²K

The requirements of the Act are met when the maximum possible thickness of insulation in technical terms is provided between the rafters over a roof space already converted into living accommodation. If the roof storey has not yet been converted, the roof assembly must be increased on the underside of the rafters as far as is necessary to satisfy the requirements.

U-value calculation:

Rafter[1]:	d [m]	λ [W/mK]	1/Λ [m²K/W]
R_{se}			0.100
Roof boarding	0.024	0.130	0.185
Rafter	0.120	0.130	0.923
Mineral fibre	0.060	0.040	1.500
Plasterboard	0.012	0.210	0.060
R_{si}			0.100
Total thermal resistance			2.868
U-value of rafter [W/m²K]			**0.35**

Infill panel[2]:	d [m]	λ [W/mK]	1/Λ [m²K/W]
R_{se}			0.100
Roof boarding	0.024	0.130	0.185
Mineral fibre	0.120	0.040	3.000
Mineral fibre	0.060	0.040	1.500
Plasterboard	0.012	0.210	0.060
R_{si}			0.100
Total thermal resistance			4.945
U-value of infill panel [W/m²K]			**0.20**

Total U-value:[3]	Share of area	U-value	Share of U-value
Rafter	0.13	0.35	0.05
Infill panel	0.87	0.20	0.18
Total U-value [W/m²K]			**0.23**

[1] b = 0.10 m
[2] b = 0.65 m
[3] Simplified calculation compared to DIN EN ISO 6924 (2003). The U-value calculated corresponds to the DIN upper limit value and is sufficiently accurate for energy performance requirements.

Insulating from inside and retaining the existing roof covering

Basically, when considering the roof insulation we must distinguish between retaining the entire roof covering or replacing it. The conditions for retaining the existing roof covering are as follows:
· existing roof covering in good condition
· the presence of a functioning secondary waterproofing/covering layer which will protect the new insulation reliably against moisture from outside
· access to the roof construction from the inside (in the ideal case an attic storey not converted into living accommodation)

Advantages:
· Saves the cost of a new roof covering.
· No scaffolding required.
· Roof remains waterproof during the work (which can be carried out regardless of the weather).
· No change to the external appearance.

Disadvantages:
· If the rafters are not deep enough for the thickness of insulation required, extra framing on the inside will be necessary (loss of internal space and height).
· If the existing secondary waterproofing/covering layer is vapour-tight (bituminous felt, PE sheeting, etc.), the building performance compatibility of the insulation measures must be carefully checked.

☐ a
The water vapour diffusion resistance index of the secondary waterproofing/covering layer has a decisive influence on the sequence of layers on the inside. This layer is often made from a very vapour-tight material, e.g. bituminous felt, or PE sheeting. Any moisture that has infiltrated the insulation can escape to the outside only very slowly when such materials are used. In such cases some of the insulation must be sacrificed in order to include an additional ventilation cavity below the secondary waterproofing/covering layer, or a vapour barrier must be added on the inside of the insulation and very carefully installed so that no moist interior air reaches the insulation. Another option is to use a vapour barrier with a variable water vapour diffusion resistance. The barrier effect of such a vapour barrier with adaptive moisture properties depends on the average ambient moisture level. During the winter the diffusion resistance rises so that only very small quantities of water vapour can infiltrate the insulation, whereas during the summer the barrier effect drops, which allows the insulation to dry out towards the inside. In all cases it is essential to assess the performance of the intended sequence of layers.

☐ b
Rigid insulating boards are not suitable for use between the rafters. Firstly, it is very time-consuming to cut these to fit exactly between the existing rafters without any gaps, and secondly, they cannot compensate for the natural swelling and shrinkage behaviour of the timber roof structure. Therefore, wedge-felt materials made from natural or mineral fibres should be installed between the rafters. Cellulose flakes represent an alternative. However, when using loose fill, make sure you create closed compartments to prevent the insulation from sagging.
Insulation in the roof space should exhibit a high heat capacity in order to ensure a better thermal phase lag and hence prevent overheating of the roof space during the summer.

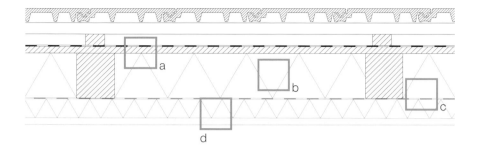

3 Isotherms before (a) and after (b) upgrading for
standard conditions to DIN 4108-2 (-5°C outside
temperature, +20°C room temperature, 50% internal r.h.)
——— 9.3°C isotherm (risk of condensation)
········ 12.6°C isotherm (risk of mould growth)
4 Heat losses and heating energy requirement in
kWh/a before and after upgrading:
losses through roof surface, floor to attic and floor
segments below storage spaces within eaves

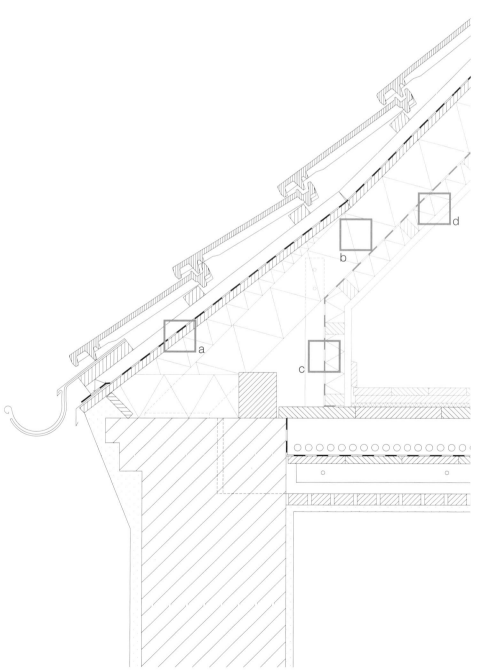

□ c
The vapour barrier also acts as the airtight membrane. Careful laying and bond-
ing at all joints and junctions is vital if convection of the interior air to the outside is
to be prevented. Convection results in
undesirable heat losses and high levels of
moisture being transported into the insulation. The vapour barrier layer should not
be interrupted if at all possible and is
therefore best positioned below purlins,
collar beams, etc. Leaving the existing
roof structure exposed is therefore not
recommended for this type of upgrade.

□ d
A second layer of insulation between the
battens at 90° to the rafters increases the
insulation thickness and eliminates the
thermal bridge effect of the rafters. In
addition, any electric cables or heating
pipes required here can be incorporated
in this layer of insulation so that they do
not penetrate the airtight vapour barrier
layer. On the inside, the layer of insulation
can be lined with plasterboard, fibrous
plasterboard or timber boarding.

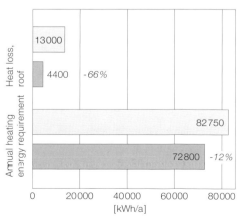

4   □ before upgrade   ■ after upgrade

5a

b

Energy Conservation Act requirements:

Requirements to be satisfied by a pitched roof after upgrading:

max. U-value 0.30 W/m²K

The requirements of the Act are met when the maximum possible thickness of insulation in technical terms is provided between the rafters over a roof space already converted into living accommodation. There is no obligation to increase the depth of the roof assembly above the rafters. If the roof storey has not yet been converted, the full amount of insulation required must be installed.

U-value calculation:

Rafter[1]:	d [m]	λ [W/mK]	1/Λ [m²K/W]
R_{se}			0.100
Roof boarding	0.024	0.130	0.185
Mineral fibre	0.120	0.040	3.000
Rafter	0.120	0.130	0.923
Wood-wool slab	0.030	0.065	0.462
Lime-cement plaster	0.015	1.000	0.017
R_{si}			0.100
Total thermal resistance			4.786
U-value of rafter [W/m²K]			**0.21**

Infill panel[2]:	d [m]	λ [W/mK]	1/Λ [m²K/W]
R_{se}			0.100
Roof boarding	0.024	0.130	0.185
Mineral fibre	0.120	0.040	3.000
Mineral fibre	0.120	0.040	3.000
Wood-wool slab	0.030	0.065	0.462
Lime-cement plaster	0.015	1.000	0.017
R_{si}			0.100
Total thermal resistance			6.863
U-value of infill panel [W/m²K]			**0.15**

Total U-value:	Share of area	U-value	Share of U-value
Rafter	0.133	0.21	0.03
Infill panel	0.867	0.15	0.13
Total U-value [W/m²K]			**0.16**

[1] b = 0.10 m
[2] b = 0.65 m

Insulating from outside and renewing the roof covering

If the roof covering needs to be refurbished anyway, or there is no functioning secondary waterproofing/covering layer, it is advisable to carry out the insulating measures from the outside.

Advantages:
- Any existing roof space conversion is not affected by the work.
- Optimum protection for the insulation against moisture from outside can be ensured.

Disadvantages:
- Higher costs (insulation, roof covering, flashings).
- Scaffolding required.
- If the rafters are not deep enough for the thickness of insulation required, extra framing on the outside will be necessary (problems concerning change of appearance and building authority approval).

☐ a
The old lining to the existing roof space conversion consists of reed mats or wood-wool slabs which are plastered on the inside. If such a plaster background has been nailed to open planking, many of the nails often penetrate into the spaces between the rafters. In such a situation first lay rigid insulating boards (e.g. EPS) – at least as thick as the longest nails – between the rafters to provide a flat backing for the subsequent vapour check and to protect it against damage.

☐ b
From the outside, lay the rolls of vapour check material parallel to and between the rafters. Turn the material up the sides of the rafters and bond it airtight to the vapour barrier material laid over the top of the rafters themselves. In doing so, it is

important that the vapour check is not stretched taut between the rafters, but rather laid with some slack so that once the insulation is installed the vapour check is pressed up hard against the rafters. This prevents warm, moist interior air from infiltrating between vapour check and rafters and reaching cooler parts of the roof construction. If the temperature drops below the dew point here, the moisture condenses and in unfavourable situations can lead to an unacceptable moisture content in the loadbearing timber structure.

This problem can be solved by laying further insulation over the rafters (as illustrated here), which means that the temperature on the top side of the rafters, too, remains considerably higher.

☐ c
It is very important that the material used for the insulation between the rafters is not a rigid insulating material, but rather a compressible mineral felt or loose fill. Only such materials ensure that the vapour barrier is pressed up hard against the rafter sides.

☐ d
The second layer of insulation above the rafters can take on various forms. In the example illustrated here, horizontal timber rails have been fitted to the rafters and the intermediate spaces filled in with mineral felt. This insulation is covered by timber boarding and a roofing felt permeable to diffusion. If non-compressible insulating materials such as rigid EPS foam boards or wood fibre insulating boards are employed, the timber rails and boarding are not required. Indeed, if specially profiled, bitumen-impregnated wood fibre insulating boards or rigid foam system boards are used, even the roofing felt can be omitted. To be on the safe side, the layers of the roof construction should be

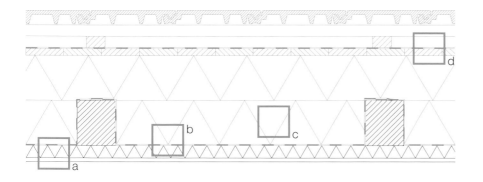

5   Isotherms before (a) and after (b) upgrading for
    standard conditions to DIN 4108-2 (-5°C outside
    temperature, +20°C room temperature, 50% inter-
    nal r.h.)
    ———   9.3°C – isotherm (risk of condensation)
    ....   12.6°C – isotherm (risk of mould growth)
6   Heat losses and heating energy requirement in
    kWh/a
    • before upgrading:
      losses through roof surface, floor to attic and
      floor segments below storage spaces within
      eaves
    • after upgrading:
      losses through thoroughly insulated roof surface
    Compared to the variation with internal insulation
    (see p. 27), the larger heated volume and the as-
    sociated greater heat loss via the gable walls has
    an effect on the heating energy requirement here.

investigated for their performance, especially when using rigid foam boards with
much improved vapour-tightness.

☐ e
If, as in this example, the roof construction is raised by adding a second layer of
insulation, it is essential to rethink and
redesign all the edge details (verge,
eaves, etc.). This is especially important
in the case of terrace and semi-detached
houses, where unsightly steps in the roof
construction can ensue. It is also important to check whether raising the ridge
and eaves levels requires the approval of
the local building authority.

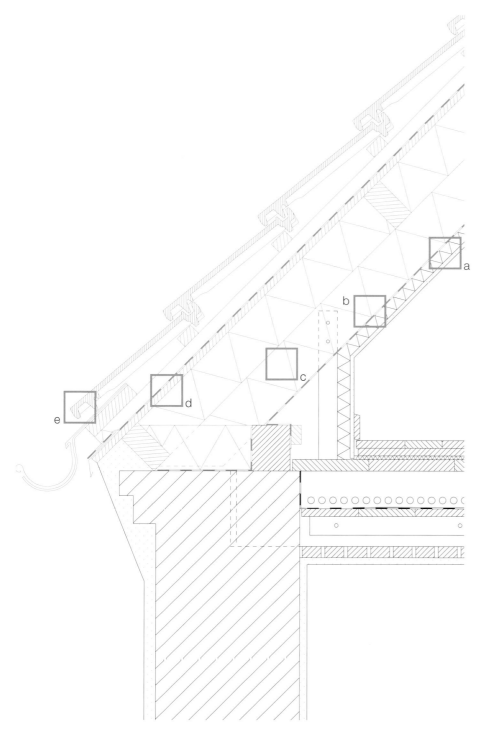

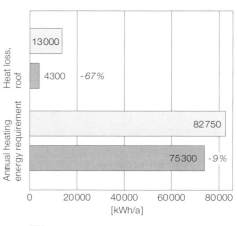

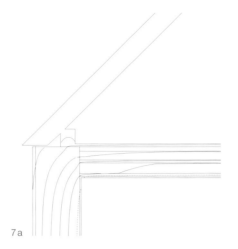

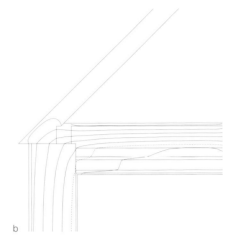

7a   b

Energy Conservation Act requirements:

Requirements to be satisfied by intermediate floors adjoining unheated interior spaces when soffit finishes are attached on the cold side, i.e. the top of the topmost floor:

max. U-value 040 W/m²K

In all other cases, i.e. for insulation on the underside of the topmost floor or insulation between the floor joists, the requirement is:

max. U-value 0.50 W/m²K

Thermal resistance of roof spaces::

It is necessary to know the thermal resistance $1/\Lambda$ of the unheated roof space when calculating the U-value of the topmost floor. This thermal resistance is specified in DIN EN ISO 6946, table 3, as follows:

Description of roof	$1/\Lambda$ [m²K/W]
1. Clay roof tiles without decking, or similar	0.060
2. Slab roof, or clay roofing tiles with building paper, decking or similar beneath tiles	0.200
3. As for 2, but with low level of emissions on-underside of roof (e.g. aluminium foil)	0.300
4. Roof with decking and building paper	0.300

U-value calculation (insulation to reinforced concrete slab):

	d [m]	λ [W/mK]	$1/\Lambda$ [m²K/W]
R_{se}			0.040
Roof space, clay tile roof			0.060
Wood-based board	0.022	0.130	0.169
Mineral fibre	0.120	0.040	3.000
Reinf. concrete slab	0.160	2.300	0.070
Lime-gypsum plaster	0.015	0.700	0.021
R_{si}			0.100
Total thermal resistance			3.460
U-value [W/m²K]			**0.29**

7 Isotherms before (a) and after (b) upgrading for standard conditions to DIN 4108-2 (-5°C outside temperature, +20°C room temperature, 50% internal r.h.)
    —— 9.3°C isotherm (risk of condensation)
    ········ 12.6°C isotherm (risk of mould growth)
8 Heat losses and heating energy requirement in kWh/a before and after upgrading:
    losses through attic floor and floor segments below storage spaces within eaves.

Insulating the topmost floor

Adding insulation to the topmost intermediate floor is one of the few mandatory construction upgrade measures specified in clause 9 of the Energy Conservation Act. A U-value of at least 0.30 W/m²K is specified for the floor construction of roof spaces that are accessible but not suitable for foot traffic. Residential buildings with a maximum of two housing units occupied by the owners themselves are the only exclusion to this upgrading obligation.

A roof space that is accessible but not suitable for foot traffic as set forth in the Act is a space that cannot be converted into living accommodation at a later date, owing to its layout. It can nevertheless be used for storage purposes. Such a roof space is normally accessed through a hatch with a ladder, and not via permanently installed stairs. In our example building this upgrading obligation concerns the floor of the accessible storage spaces within the eaves and the attic above the roof space conversion.

When insulating the floor, pay special attention to the access openings to these roof spaces. What is important here is not the insulation value of the door or hatch concerned, but rather its airtightness. The stack effect can lead to large amounts of warm interior air escaping without any noticeable draughts because the cold air tends to enter through leaks in the floors below.

In the following we distinguish between adding a new floor construction with insulating felts or loose fill, and a floor construction "floated" on rigid insulating materials.

☐ a

Remove the existing timber floorboards in order to use the existing voids between the timber joists for insulating purposes. Fill the void above the loose fill on the

sound boarding with an insulating felt material made from mineral or natural fibres, or a loose fill material, e.g. cellulose flakes, up to the top of the timber joists. Either plastic sheeting or building paper with glued joints serves as a vapour barrier and airtight membrane. Lay timber rails at 90° to the joists and again fill the spaces between with insulating material. Cover this with simple floorboards or other flooring-grade boards.

☐ b

Use a batten and a preformed compressible strip to clamp the vapour barrier and airtight membrane tightly to the top of the masonry external wall.

☐ c

In the case of a timber joist floor, make sure that outside air cannot enter the void beneath the sound boarding through leaking joints at the joist supports. If this happens, the overlying thermal insulation becomes useless in certain windy conditions. Therefore, add a strip of sheeting on top of the masonry and cover it with further, loose-fill insulation material so that the thermal bridge effect at the top of the wall is reduced as far as possible and the ends of the timber joists are no longer at risk of rotting caused by condensation.

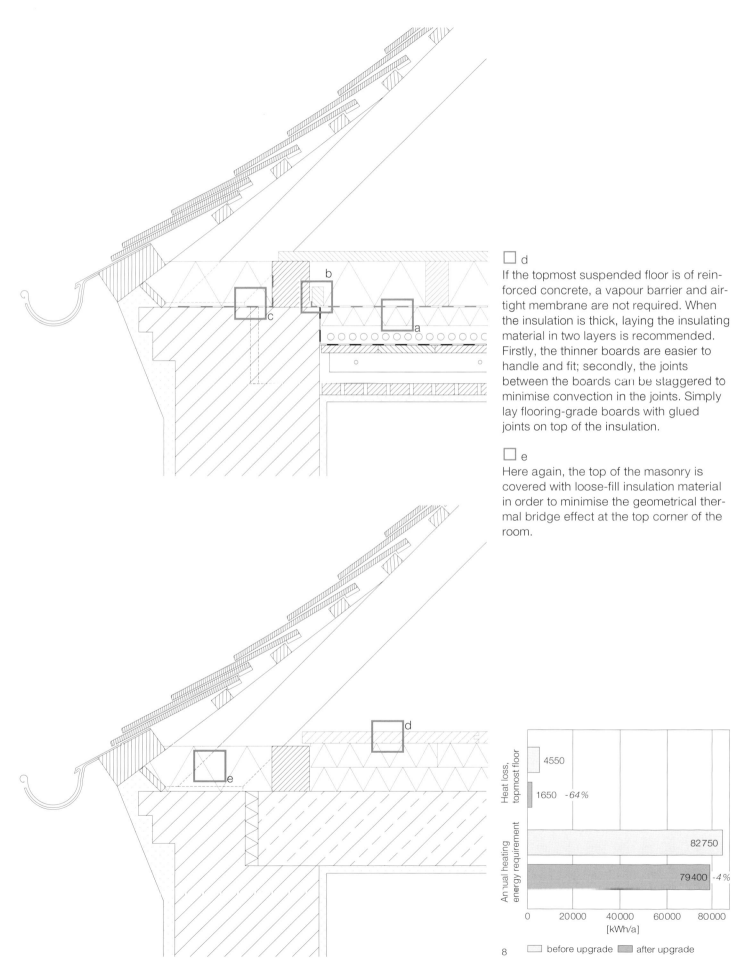

□ d

If the topmost suspended floor is of reinforced concrete, a vapour barrier and airtight membrane are not required. When the insulation is thick, laying the insulating material in two layers is recommended. Firstly, the thinner boards are easier to handle and fit; secondly, the joints between the boards can be staggered to minimise convection in the joints. Simply lay flooring-grade boards with glued joints on top of the insulation.

□ e

Here again, the top of the masonry is covered with loose-fill insulation material in order to minimise the geometrical thermal bridge effect at the top corner of the room.

Heat loss, topmost floor
4550
1650 -64%

Annual heating energy requirement
82750
79400 -4%

0   20000   40000   60000   80000
[kWh/a]

8   □ before upgrade   ■ after upgrade

31

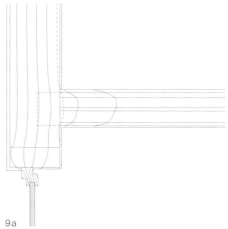

9a

b

Energy Conservation Act requirements:

Requirements for external walls on which cladding is attached to the outside or layers of insulation are installed:

max. U-value 0.35 W/m²K

If the render is renewed on an existing external wall with a U-value > 0.9 W/m²K, there is an obligation to maintain a limit value of 0.35 W/m²K with the help of additional insulating measures.

U-value calculation:	d [m]	λ [W/mK]	1/Λ [m²K/W]
R_{se}			0.040
Synthetic resin render	0.005	0.700	0.007
Rigid PS foam	0.120	0.035	3.429
Lime-cement render	0.025	0.870	0.029
Masonry	0.300	0.610	0.492
Lime-gypsum plaster	0.015	0.700	0.021
R_{si}			0.130
Total thermal resistance			4.148
U-value of external wall [W/m²K]			**0.24**

U-value of new window: nom. value according to DIN 4108-4	
U-value of glazing (U_g): solar-control glass [W/m²K]	1.1
U-value of frame (U_f): wooden frame [W/m²K]	1.8
U-value of window ($U_{w, BW}$) [W/m²K]	**1.5**

9 Isotherms before (a) and after (b) upgrading for standard conditions to DIN 4108-2 (-5°C outside temperature, +20°C room temperature, 50% internal r.h.)
——— 9.3°C isotherm (risk of condensation)
········ 12.6°C isotherm (risk of mould growth)
10 Heat losses and heating energy requirement in kWh/a before and after upgrading:
external wall losses including windows

Thermal insulation composite system plus new windows

In most cases, adding insulation externally to the opaque facade surfaces in the form of a thermal insulation composite system represents the most effective and economic insulating measure. On the one hand, the opaque facades of residential buildings almost always represent the larger share of the building envelope, and on the other, the U-values of existing monolithic external walls are usually much poorer than the multi-layer roof and suspended floor constructions.

Advantages:
· The heat-storage mass of the solid external wall is still effective for the interior.
· The majority of constructional thermal bridges can be eliminated, the geometrical thermal bridges substantially minimised.
· All heat losses due to, for example, poorly insulated heating pipes buried in external walls, benefit the interior.

Disadvantages:
· Thicker walls (problems related to appearance and building authority approval).
· All junctions between facade and other components must be redesigned and adapted.
· The facade is more susceptible to mechanical damage and algae.
· Replacing the windows at a later date is very difficult.

It is therefore advisable to install new windows at the same time as a thermal insulation composite system. This allows the new windows to be installed in the best position within the depth of the wall, in terms of the thermal performance and in conjunction with the thermal insulation composite system. The shallow outer reveal results in a customary facade appearance.

☐ a
Set the new window further forward, flush with the old render and therefore as close as possible to the new thermal insulation. This avoids excessive discontinuity of the insulation plane, which is disadvantageous from the thermal point of view. The new thermal insulation covers the joint between window surround and masonry, and therefore mitigates the thermal bridge effect.

☐ b
Insulating boards and rendering system form one unit and must be coordinated with each other. The most common thermal insulation composite systems are as follows:
· rigid polystyrene or polyurethane foam boards with organic or inorganic rendering systems (building materials class B1)
· mineral fibre boards with inorganic rendering system (building materials class A)
· cork, wood-fibre or reed insulating boards with inorganic rendering systems (building materials class B2)
· mineral foam boards with inorganic rendering system (building materials class A)

The fire protection requirements have a direct effect on the choice of insulating materials and renders. The permissible building materials class of a thermal insulation composite system depends on the height h of the topmost floor above the adjoining ground level:

· min. B2 (flammable) for h < 7 m
· min. B1 (not readily flammable) for h = 7–22 m
· A (incombustible) for h > 22 m

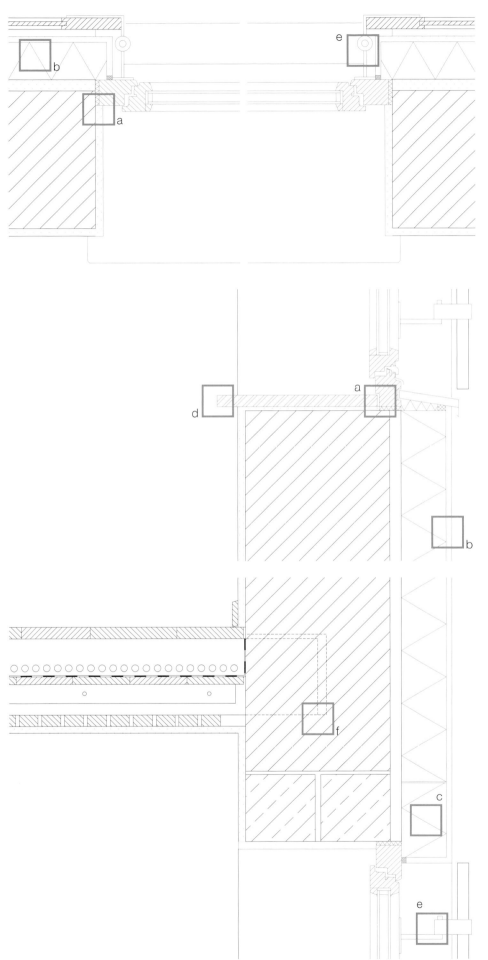

☐ c

Thermal insulation composite systems with rigid PS or PUR foam boards >100 mm thick represent a special case in terms of fire protection. A class A insulating strip must be attached directly above all window lintels. It must extend at least 200 mm vertically and 300 mm to both sides of the window. The purpose of this is to protect the escape route through the window in the event of a fire from molten insulating material.

☐ d

The new position of the windows within the depth of the external wall increases the depth of the inner reveals, necessitating additional plaster. A new window board is also necessary. In occupied buildings such measures are often a hindrance to progress.

☐ e

Existing window shutters will require new hardware and may need to be adapted to fit the slightly smaller clear opening size of the new window. The new position of the window within the depth of the wall rules out reusing an existing roller shutter and accompanying casings.

☐ f

The external thermal insulation has a positive effect on the supports for timber joist floors. After the insulation has been attached, the wall temperatures are much higher and condensation is now extremely unlikely in this area.

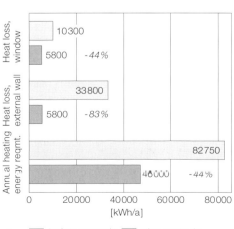

		[kWh/a]
Heat loss, window	10300	
	5800	−44%
Heat loss, external wall	33800	
	5800	−83%
Annual heating energy reqmt.	82750	
	46000	−44%

0   20000   40000   60000   80000
[kWh/a]

10   ☐ before upgrade   ▢ after upgrade

33

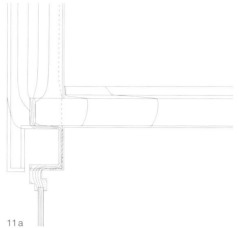
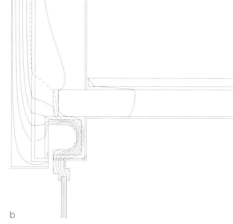

11a   b

Requirements for external walls on which cladding is attached to the outside or layers of insulation are installed:

max. U-value 0.35 W/m²K

If the render is renewed on an existing external wall with a U-value >0.9 W/m²K, there is an obligation to maintain a limit value of 0.35 W/m²K with the help of additional insulating measures.

Requirements for roller shutter housings:

The Energy Conservation Act does not specify any special requirements for roller shutter casings. However, when calculating the transmission heat losses, the facade areas of roller shutter casings must be shown separately and considered with their own U-value when the Act's global thermal bridge surcharge of 0.10 W/m²K is assumed.
According to the minimum requirements of DIN 4108-2, or the 1995 Thermal Insulation Act, the U-values for roller shutter housings are normally:

U-value (installed pre-1995)	1.39 W/m²K
U-value (installed post-1995)	0.60 W/m²K

If the optimised thermal bridge surcharge of 0.05 W/m²K is assumed, or the thermal bridges are analysed individually, the roller shutter casings may be added to the area of the external wall.
If it is desired to assume the optimised thermal bridge surcharge, the design rules according to DIN 4108 supplement 2 must be satisfied: approx. 60 mm thermal insulation of type WLG 040 must be provided on the contact surfaces between roller shutter casings and interior and between roller shutter casings and suspended floor.

U-value calculation:	d [m]	λ [W/mK]	1/Λ [m²K/W]
R_{se}			0.040
Synthetic resin render	0.005	0.700	0.007
Rigid PS foam	0.120	0.035	3.429
Lime-cement render	0.025	0.870	0.029
Masonry	0.300	0.610	0.492
Lime-gypsum plaster	0.015	0.700	0.021
R_{si}			0.130
Total thermal resistance			4.148
U-value of external wall [W/m²K]			**0.24**

11 Isotherms before (a) and after (b) upgrading for standard conditions to DIN 4108-2 (-5°C outside temperature, +20°C room temperature, 50% internal r.h.)
    —— 9.3°C isotherm (risk of condensation)
    .... 12.6°C isotherm (risk of mould growth))
12 Heat losses and heating energy requirement in kWh/a before and after upgrading:
    external wall losses

Thermal insulation composite system plus new windows with roller shutters

In the majority of cases the windows are renewed when a thermal insulation composite system is installed. This allows the windows to be set in the best position from the energy performance viewpoint, i.e. flush with the outer face of the original masonry (see pp. 32–33). However, the following line of reasoning may lead to the original position of the windows being retained, indeed even the existing windows themselves:

· The windows are in excellent condition and can be improved (in thermal terms) by simple means.
· The windows have already been replaced.
· The existing roller shutters and their associated casings are to be reused.
· Costly additional plasterwork and replacement of the window boards inside is to be avoided.

In architectural terms, this approach leads to much deeper outer reveals, which may alter the appearance of the building considerably.
The junction between the thermal insulation composite system and the existing windows requires special attention.

☐ a
Make sure the existing windows have been properly installed, i.e. are permanently airtight. It may also be necessary to improve the external junction between window surround and masonry. This involves filling the joints again or covering them with suitable preformed sealing strips. Simply filling them with PUR spray foam does not constitute a reliable sealing solution because once it cures, the hard foam cannot accommodate any movement of the window surround and is therefore liable to crack.

☐ b
The reveal itself must be insulated on the outside. If the requirements regarding the treatment of thermal bridges according to DIN 4108 supplement 2 are to be met, then the reveals require ≥30 mm thick insulating boards of type WLG 040. In some cases it may be necessary to remove the existing render to the reveals first in order to create space for the additional insulation.

☐ c
Replace existing sheet metal window sills to accommodate the additional insulation. Solder or weld together the turned-up edges at the sides and back of the window sill so that no water can infiltrate the thermal insulation composite system during driving rain; the aluminium sections that are simply plugged onto the window sill to form the terminations at both sides are not reliable enough. At the sides in particular, the sheet metal must be separated from the render of the thermal insulation composite system by a waterbar or a stop bead. Otherwise, the different thermal expansion behaviour of the materials can lead to restraining stresses between window sill and render which considerably increases the risk of cracking.

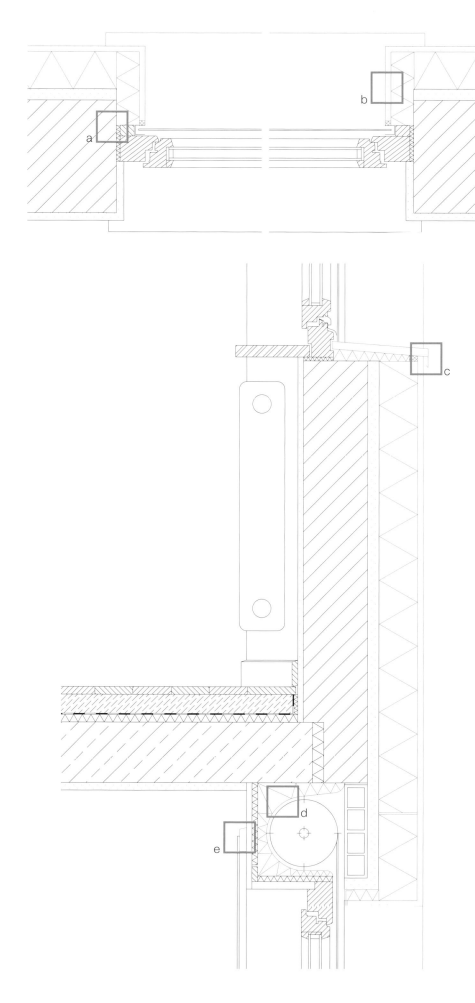

☐ d
The thermal insulation composite system extends over the roller shutter casing. In order to guarantee sufficiently high surface temperatures on the inside of the roller shutter casing, thermal improvement is usually necessary. Various manufacturers already supply prefabricated polystyrene foam inserts for insulating the existing voids within the roller shutter casing. If there is insufficient space for insulation plus rolled-up shutter between spindle and casing, it may be necessary to replace the existing slats by thinner ones which can be rolled up in a smaller space. An airtight seal around the inspection opening is particularly important when upgrading roller shutter housings.

☐ e
Since the opening for the shutter operating cord represents a direct link between interior and exterior, it should be sealed as far as possible by installing brush seals.

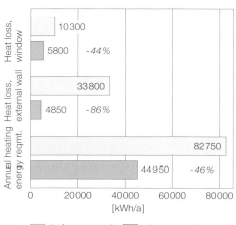

12   ☐ before upgrade   ▨ after upgrade

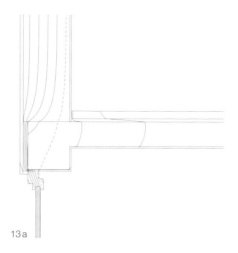

13a   b

Energy Conservation Act requirements:

Requirements for external walls on which cladding is attached to the outside or layers of insulation are installed:

max. U-value 0.35 W/m²K

U-value calculation:	d [m]	λ [W/mK]	1/Λ [m²K/W]
R_{se}			0.130
Wood-based board	0.020	0.130	0.154
Mineral fibre	0.160	0.040	4.000
Lime-cement render	0.025	0.870	0.029
Masonry	0.300	0.610	0.492
Lime-gypsum plaster	0.015	0.700	0.021
R_{si}			0.130
Total thermal resistance			4.956
U-value [W/m²K]			**0.20**

U-value of new window: nominal value according to DIN 4108-4	
U-value of glazing (U_g): solar-control glass [W/m²K]	1.1
U-value of frame (U_f): wooden frame [W/m²K]	1.8
U-value window ($U_{w, BW}$) [W/m²K]	**1.5**

13   Isotherms before (a) and after (b) upgrading for standard conditions to DIN 4108-2 (-5°C outside temperature, +20°C room temperature, 50% internal r.h.)
     ——— 9.3°C isotherm (risk of condensation)
     ········ 12.6°C isotherm (risk of mould growth)
14   Heat losses and heating energy requirement in kWh/a before and after upgrading:
external wall losses including windows

Thermal insulation with ventilation cavity and new windows

The biggest change to the appearance of a facade is when the refurbishment work includes thermal insulation plus a ventilation cavity behind the cladding. However, depending on the brief, this may represent a particularly appealing architectural challenge.

Advantages:
· Best building performance characteristics thanks to separation of thermal insulation and weatherproof layers.
· Maximum freedom of choice for cladding material and facade design.

Disadvantages:
· High costs.
· High design input.
· Large depth of construction (space requirement).

☐ a
The new windows have a wider window surround, which means they have to be fixed to the outside of the masonry wall. They are supported on individual brackets and lie completely in the external insulation plane, which further reduces the thermal bridge effect in the window reveal. An airtight joint between window and masonry is guaranteed, the proportion of the frame protruding into the existing opening can be minimised.

☐ b
The facade cladding has to be fixed to a framework, whose members are best spaced to suit the width of the insulating material. To minimise thermal bridges associated with this framing, it is best to construct this in the form of two layers of rails at 90° to each other. The thermal insulation between the framing members need not be rigid; indeed with suitable edge details and boarding on the outside,

it can also be in the form of a loose fill.

☐ c
The insulating material used may require the framework to be completely covered with boards or planks. In order to be able to exploit the building performance advantages of the ventilation cavity, the board material should be highly permeable to vapour. Together with the overlying airtight membrane (open to diffusion), this permeability should be less than the diffusion resistance of the existing external wall.

☐ d
Possible cladding materials are as follows:

· fibre-cement sheets
· compressed synthetic resin-bonded wood-based products
· timber sheathing and shakes/shingles
· wood-based products (limited options)
· sheet metal
· stone slabs
· clay-tile elements
· render background boards (e.g. calcium silicate sheets)

When fixing the respective cladding material to the supporting framework, take into account that the cladding is subjected to large temperature fluctuations. The resulting changes in length should not lead to unacceptable restraining stresses or distortion.

☐ e
The design of the joints depends on both the cladding material selected and the type of supporting framework. Adequate ventilation behind the cladding is achieved by open joints on all sides. However, this presumes that the horizontal edges of the cladding material are unaffected by water, likewise the framework itself. In

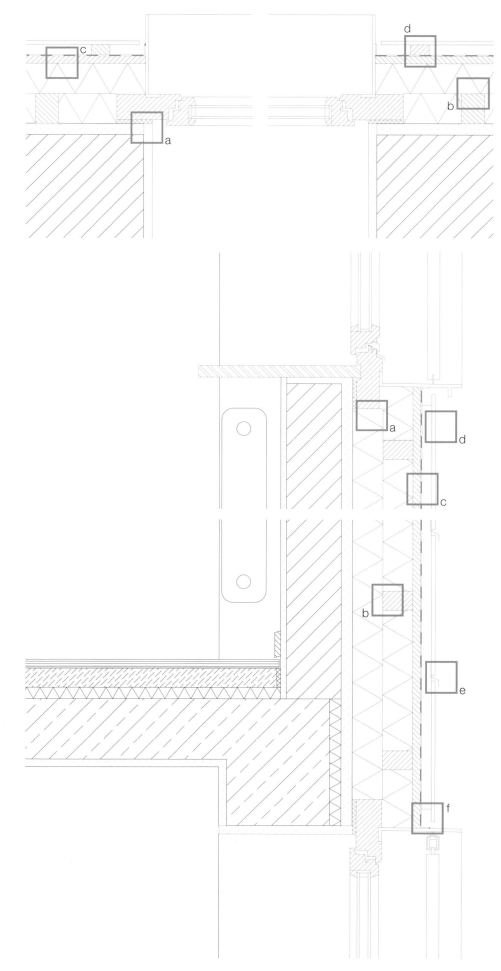

many cases simply concealing the horizontal joints by overlapping or using Z-sections is sufficient, whereas the vertical joints can remain open. This minimises the ingress of water during driving rain and water that does penetrate can simply drain down the rear face or dry out.

☐ f
Careful detailing is essential for all joints and junctions, e.g. at the window reveals. The pattern of the joints in the cladding should be coordinated with the openings as far as possible. If the ventilation cavity is interrupted, make sure that vents are included above and below the interruption.

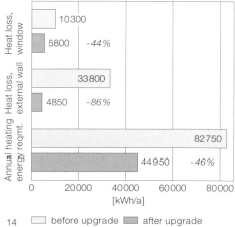

14 ☐ before upgrade ▨ after upgrade

15 Isotherms before (a) and after (b) upgrading for standard conditions to DIN 4108-2 (-5°C outside temperature, +20°C room temperature, 50% internal r.h.)
————— 9.3°C isotherm (risk of condensation)
········· 12.6°C isotherm (risk of mould growth)
16 Heat losses and heating energy requirement in kWh/a before and after upgrading:
external wall losses including windows

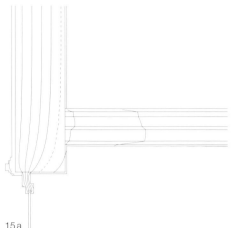

15a b

Energy Conservation Act requirements:

Requirements for external walls on which lining or boarding is attached to the inside:

max. U-value 0.45 W/m²K

Compared to forms of construction insulated on the outside, external walls with internal insulation suffer from severe thermal bridges. In order to achieve realistic results for the associated calculations, the thermal bridge heat-loss coefficient has therefore been doubled to 0.20 W/m²K, like in the German Energy Agency field trials (see p. 24). The Act itself does not include such a provision.

U-value calculation for external wall:

	d [m]	λ [W/mK]	1/Λ [m²K/W]
R_{se}			0.040
Lime-cement render	0.025	0.870	0.029
Masonry	0.300	0.610	0.492
Lime-gypsum plaster	0.015	0.700	0.021
Mineral fibre	0.060	0.040	1.500
Plasterboard	0.015	0.250	0.060
R_{si}			0.130
Total thermal resistance			2.272
U-value [W/m²K]			**0.44**

U-value of individual window:
Calculation according to DIN EN ISO 10077-1

U-value of inner leaf [W/m²K] (nominal value to DIN 4108-4)	1.5
Total thermal resistance [m²K/W]	0.667
U-value of outer leaf [W/m²K] (nominal value to DIN 4108-4)	4.5
Total thermal resistance [m²K/W]	0.222

U-value of double window:

	1/Λ [m²K/W]
Inner window	0.667
$-R_{se}$	−0.040
Cavity > 100 mm	0.173
$-R_{si}$	−0.130
Outer window	0.222
Total thermal resistance	0.892
Total U-value ($U_{w, BW}$) [W/m²K]	**1.12**

Internal insulation plus upgrading of existing single glazing

When external walls are insulated on the inside, the external appearance of the building remains unchanged. Internal insulation is therefore mainly used in conjunction with stucco or facing brickwork facades worthy of preservation.

Advantages:
· No change to the external appearance.
· No building authority approval problems.
· Partial (room-by-room) external wall insulation is possible.
· Low-cost.

Disadvantages:
· The heat-storage mass of the solid external wall cannot be utilised.
· Risk to the building fabric because the loadbearing external walls experience a substantial drop in temperature.
· Severe thermal bridge effects around junctions with internal walls and suspended floors.
· Building performance problems, primarily in the vicinity of timber joist floors.
· Risk of freezing for water and heating pipes buried in external walls.

Placing the thermal insulation on the warm side of a heavyweight component ignores tried-and-tested rules of construction, and this calls for thorough building performance investigations in advance and very careful workmanship. In order to avoid high relative humidity during the heating period and, hence, a risk of moisture damage, it is advisable to install controlled ventilation and internal insulation at the same time.

☐ a
Always include an internal vapour barrier with internal insulation. It is very difficult for any moisture that infiltrates the insulation to escape to the outside because the diffusion resistance of the plastered and rendered masonry wall is relatively high. Apart from that, the inert masonry heats up only very slowly as the external temperature rises, which means that any drying processes occur only after a considerable delay.
However, the vapour barrier can be omitted if a vapour-tight insulating material (e.g. cellular glass) is used, or if occasional condensation at the boundary between internal insulation and masonry will not cause any harm.
Nevertheless, it is essential to ensure that the wall can fully dry out again during periods of dry weather, and that moisture-resistant insulating material is used (e.g. mineral foam, rigid PUR foam or calcium silicate sheets).

☐ b
A supporting framework – e.g. timber rails – for the inner lining is required in the case of non-rigid insulating materials. All rigid insulating materials can be bonded directly to the inside face of the external wall with suitable mortar or adhesive. Such insulating materials include different types of sandwich panels made from a core of rigid PS foam or mineral wool, mounted on various materials which are supplied with an integral vapour barrier.

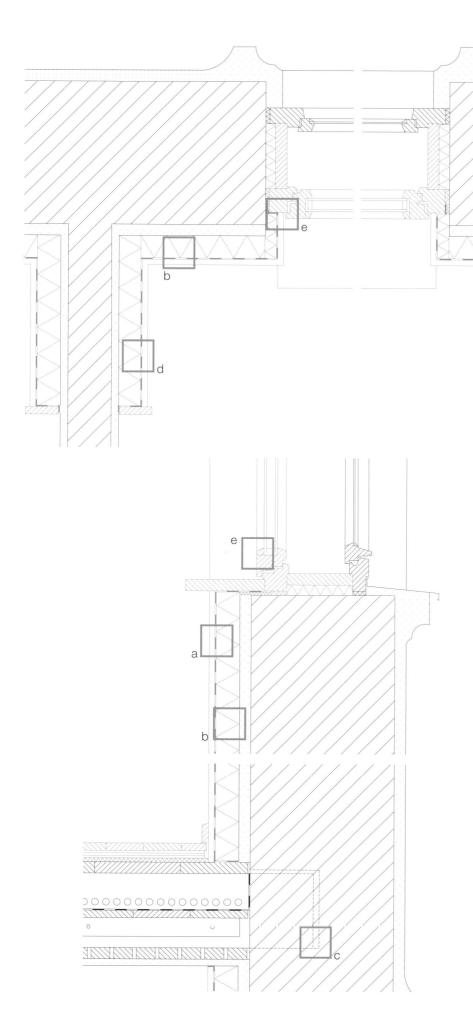

☐ c

Timber joist floors supported in pockets in the external walls require special attention. Once internal insulation has been installed, the temperature of the loadbearing external wall drops dramatically, and in most cases below the dew point of the interior air around the joist supports. Condensation in this area can raise the moisture content at the joist ends to such a level that rotting and, finally, failure of the suspended floor is possible. Exposing the ends of timber joist and beam supports and filling all voids with PUR spray foam has been shown to be worthwhile in order to minimise the air convection currents between voids in the floor construction and supports.

☐ d

Owing to the severe thermal bridge effect resulting when internal walls interlock with the external masonry, it is necessary to extend the insulation into the room approx. 500 mm. Similarly, add a strip of perimeter insulation to the soffits of all reinforced concrete floors that are supported on external walls. Such perimeter insulation is not necessary with timber joist floors because the thermal bridge effect is much less significant.

☐ e

Retain the existing single-glazed windows to preserve the appearance of the building. On the inside, add new double-glazed windows in wooden frames. The old windows are not airtight and so condensation is not a problem even when the external temperature is low.

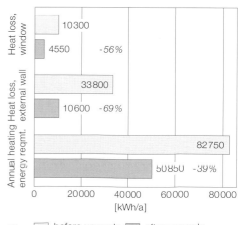

| | before upgrade | after upgrade |

Heat loss, window: 10300 / 4550 −56%
Heat loss, external wall: 33800 / 10600 −69%
Annual heating energy reqmt.: 82750 / 50850 −39%

16

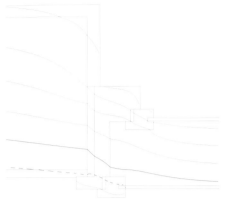

17 a

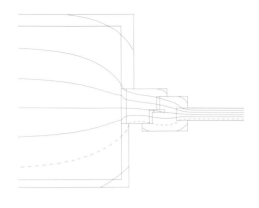

b

Energy Conservation Act requirements:

Requirements to be satisfied by windows and glass
doors in the external wall which are completely replaced or upgraded with secondary glazing:

max. U-value 1.70 W/m²K standard case
max. U-value 2.00 W/m²K special glass
max. U-value 1.90 W/m²K curtain wall
max. U-value 2.30 W/m²K curtain wall +
      special glass

Requirements to be satisfied by the glass if this is
replaced in existing windows and glass doors in the
external wall:

max. U-value 1.50 W/m²K standard case
max. U-value 1.60 W/m²K special glass

German Energy Agency reference values

The following thermal transmittance values have been
compiled as an aid within the scope of the German
Energy Agency field trials to establish a practical energy certificate:

Type of glass, type of frame	U-value [W/m²K]		g-value
Single glazing	$U_g =$	5.8	0.87
- in wooden frame	$U_w =$	5.0	
Double glazing or 2 single-glazed windows	$U_g =$	2.8	0.75
- in aluminium frame without thermal break	$U_w =$	4.3	
- in aluminium frame with thermal break	$U_w =$	3.2	
- in plastic frame	$U_w =$	3.0	
- in wooden frame	$U_w =$	2.7	
Double glazing with solar-control glass	$U_g =$	1.1	0.60
- in plastic or aluminium-frame ($U_f < 2$ W/m²K)	$U_w =$	1.9	
- in wooden frame	$U_w =$	1.6	
Triple glazing with solar-control glass	$U_g =$	0.7	0.50
- in improved wooden frame ($U_f < 1.5$ W/m²K)	$U_w =$	1.2	
- in passive-energy-house frame ($U_f < 0.8$ W/m²K)	$U_w =$	0.9	

Upgrading measures for existing windows

Instead of simply replacing existing windows, there are various ways in which
their energy efficiency can be improved.
However, this approach depends heavily
on the condition of the windows and the
building performance boundary conditions.

Advantages:
- Little or no change to the external
  appearance (and hence no building
  authority approval problems).
- No demolition work required.
- Typically low-cost.

Disadvantages:
- Standard of insulation and airtightness
  may not match that of new windows.

☐ a
Attaching weatherstripping
Retrofitted weatherstripping can reduce
ventilation heat losses considerably,
especially in the case of well-preserved
Kastenfenster or older double-glazed windows with tropical hardwood frames. One
option available ist a self-adhesive strip,
which, although it can be attached by the
layperson, exhibits only a very limited
durability. A much more permanent solution is to cut grooves in the window
frames for the standard sealing profiles.
This is a good opportunity to increase the
gap slightly so that the window can still
be closed without force after the weatherstripping has been installed. It is usually
sufficient to seal the inner sash in the
case of double windows.
Leaving the old glass in place can be
advantageous, despite its poor U-value. If
the internal surface temperature of the
glass is lower than that of the external
wall, especially near the reveal, condensation will first form on the glass, where it
is clearly visible. Attentive occupants will

notice this and open the window for ventilation before the condensation starts to
collect in the external wall itself, where –
initially unnoticed – it can lead to mould
growth. Therefore, refraining from the
installation of high-quality solar-control
glass can lead to improved control over
the interior climate.

☐ b
Replacing the glass
For newer windows already fitted with
weatherstripping, it is often sufficient to
replace the glass in order to improve the
energy performance. The frame section of
standard double-glazed wooden windows
have changed only slightly over the past
20 years. Over the same period, however,
the U-value of the glass used has been
more than halved, from an average of
2.6 W/m²K to 1.1 W/m²K, which means
there is enormous energy-saving potential
in glass, particularly if the glazed surface
area is large. The situation is different for
windows with metal and plastic frames.
The thermal quality of such frames has
increased considerably over the years.

☐ c
Installing renovation windows
In this solution the old window surround
serves as a fixing for a new window. To
do this, cut back the existing window surround in situ to a minimum size and fit a
new, two-part window surround on top of
this. Such renovation windows are available with plastic or wood/aluminium
frames. They are very popular owing to
their simple installation which does not
require altering the reveals or window
boards/sills. However, if the old window
surround is not airtight, simply adding a
new window will not eliminate such problems.
The actual insulating characteristics of
the new window surround are also heavily
dependent on the quality of workmanship.

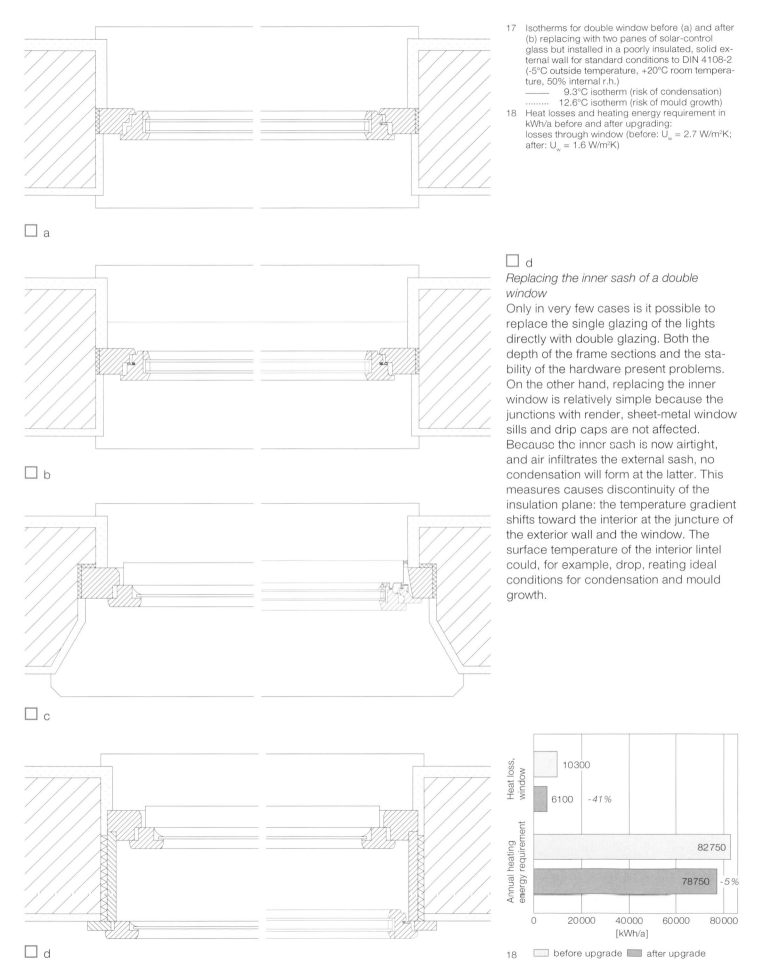

☐ a

☐ b

☐ c

☐ d

17 Isotherms for double window before (a) and after
(b) replacing with two panes of solar-control
glass but installed in a poorly insulated, solid external wall for standard conditions to DIN 4108-2
(-5°C outside temperature, +20°C room temperature, 50% internal r.h.)
——— 9.3°C isotherm (risk of condensation)
········ 12.6°C isotherm (risk of mould growth)
18 Heat losses and heating energy requirement in
kWh/a before and after upgrading:
losses through window (before: U_w = 2.7 W/m²K;
after: U_w = 1.6 W/m²K)

☐ d

*Replacing the inner sash of a double
window*

Only in very few cases is it possible to
replace the single glazing of the lights
directly with double glazing. Both the
depth of the frame sections and the stability of the hardware present problems.
On the other hand, replacing the inner
window is relatively simple because the
junctions with render, sheet-metal window
sills and drip caps are not affected.
Because the inner sash is now airtight,
and air infiltrates the external sash, no
condensation will form at the latter. This
measures causes discontinuity of the
insulation plane: the temperature gradient
shifts toward the interior at the juncture of
the exterior wall and the window. The
surface temperature of the interior lintel
could, for example, drop, reating ideal
conditions for condensation and mould
growth.

Heat loss, window

10300

6100   *-41%*

Annual heating energy requirement

82750

78750 *-5%*

0   20000   40000   60000   80000
[kWh/a]

18   ☐ before upgrade ■ after upgrade

41

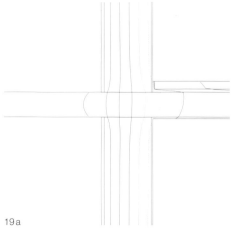

19a

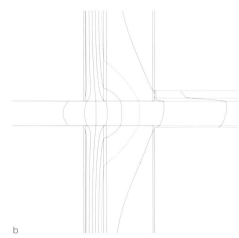

b

Energy Conservation Act requirements:

Requirements to be satisfied by entrance doors that are completely replaced:

max. U-value 2.9 W/m²K

There are basically three ways of incorporating existing thermal bridges in the energy performance calculations according to the Act:

Firstly, multiply the thermal bridge heat-loss coefficient of

0.10 W/m²K

by the total area of the building envelope and add this to the other transmission heat losses. This approach is always permissible. However, when a detailed analysis of thermal bridges is not carried out, the penalty is an unrealistically high surcharge.

Secondly, multiply the thermal bridge heat-loss coefficient of

0.05 W/m²K

by the total area of the building envelope and add this to the other transmission heat losses. This approach is only permissible for designs in conformance with DIN 4108 supplement 2. Such designs are mandatory when the energy performance calculations according to the Act are to be carried out with the simplified method (heating period audit). In the case of deviating designs, proof of equivalence to designs to DIN 4108 supplement 2 must be furnished.

Thirdly, an exact calculation of the transmission heat loss requirements based on the individual, linear thermal transmittance values at thermal bridges according to DIN EN ISO 10211-1

is always permissible. However, this approach requires a great deal of work. The lengths of all thermal bridges must be determined and the associated thermal transmittance values worked out.

19 Isotherms before (a) and after (b) attaching a thermal insulation composite system with a cantilevering reinforced concrete balcony slab for standard conditions to DIN 4108-2 (-5°C outside temperature, +20°C room temperature, 50% internal r.h.)
.... 9.3°C isotherm (risk of condensation)
———— 12.6°C isotherm (risk of mould growth)
20 Heat losses and heating energy requirement in kWh/a before and after upgrading:
losses through entrance doors, external wall and via thermal bridges over the entire building (thermal bridge heat-loss coefficient reduced from 0.10 to 0.05 W/m²K because balcony slab cut off flush with masonry)

New balcony, thermal insulation composite system and new entrance door

When carrying out energy performance calculations in accordance with the Energy Conservation Act, a cantilevering reinforced concrete balcony without a thermal break makes it impossible to reduce the thermal bridge heat-loss coefficient of 0.10 W/m²K to the 0.05 W/m²K required for optimised designs to DIN 4108 supplement 2. This thermal bridge is so severe, that even the proof of equivalence permitted for the balcony designs specified in the DIN standard is impossible. If the optimised thermal bridge heat-loss coefficient of 0.05 W/m²K is to be assumed, the balcony slab must be cut off flush with the external wall before attaching the thermal insulation composite system. Afterwards, the balcony is replaced by an independent timber or steel construction erected in front of the building or supported/suspended from individual fixings on the facade.

Advantages:
• Balcony design with virtually no thermal bridges.
• No risk of mould growth along edges of ceilings or floors in the adjacent rooms.
• The balconies can be enlarged within the scope of the project, which leads to improved living standards.

Disadvantages:
• Very expensive and involves considerable work.

If there is mould growing along the edges of ceilings and/or floors in the adjacent rooms owing to the thermal bridge effect of a cantilevering balcony slab without a thermal break, simply adding external thermal insulation will improve the situation. Costly and elaborate insulation to the balcony slab, or complete removal, is unnecessary. As the above thermal

bridge simulations show, the temperature gradient shifts outwards to such an extent that the post-refurbishment internal surface temperatures lie well above the critical temperatures. The only potential problems are at the bottom of the reveals to the balcony door, which may require internal insulation locally.

To do this, remove the plaster at the bottom of the reveals and replace it, for example, with calcium silicate sheets with a thickness equal to that of the plaster. The internal surface temperatures then lie above the critical range for mould growth. And as this is only a very small area of internal insulation, no further building performance problems are to be expected. Following the insulating measures, however, the thermal bridge has a more noticeable energy performance effect. The additional heat loss is then 0.62 W/mK, which – per linear metre – corresponds to the heat loss of approx. 2.5 m² of upgraded wall surface.

☐ a
Use a sandwich panel for the new entrance door in order to reduce the heat loss per unit area. External doors are thin, two-dimensional building components which are subjected to severe thermal fluctuations and stresses. To improve their dimensional stability, additional steel sections are incorporated in the sandwich construction and sheet steel or aluminium used as facings on both sides of the core of insulation.

☐ b
To ensure adequate airtightness at the entrance door, the door leaf has a peripheral double rebate with two sealing levels.

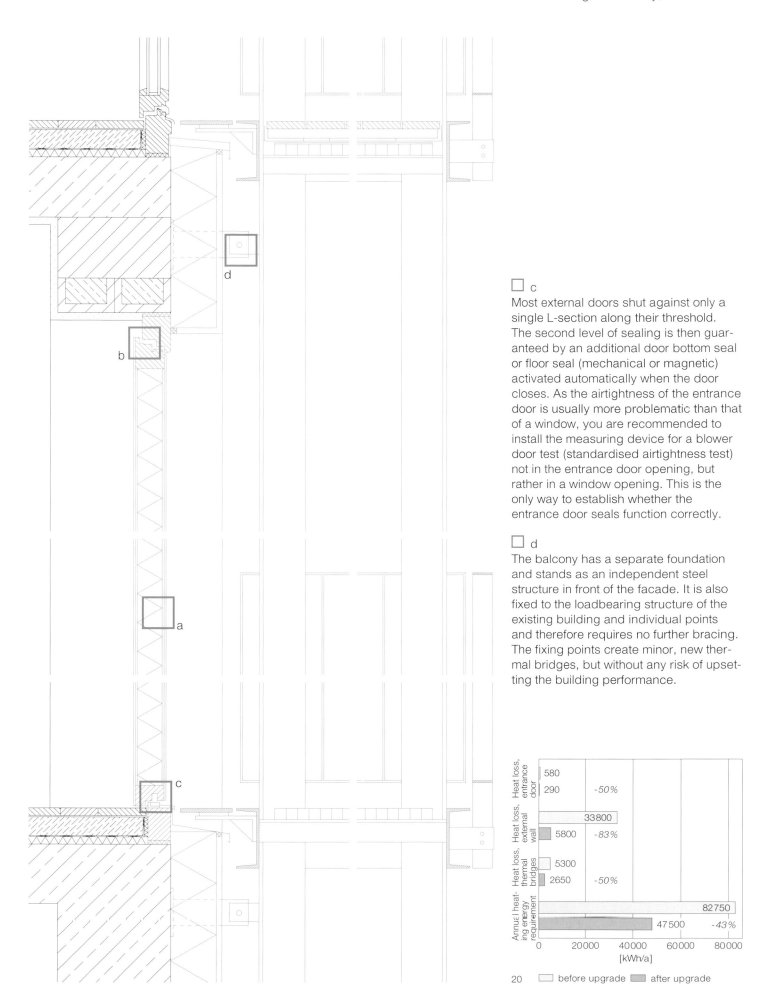

☐ c

Most external doors shut against only a single L-section along their threshold. The second level of sealing is then guaranteed by an additional door bottom seal or floor seal (mechanical or magnetic) activated automatically when the door closes. As the airtightness of the entrance door is usually more problematic than that of a window, you are recommended to install the measuring device for a blower door test (standardised airtightness test) not in the entrance door opening, but rather in a window opening. This is the only way to establish whether the entrance door seals function correctly.

☐ d

The balcony has a separate foundation and stands as an independent steel structure in front of the facade. It is also fixed to the loadbearing structure of the existing building and individual points and therefore requires no further bracing. The fixing points create minor, new thermal bridges, but without any risk of upsetting the building performance.

20 ☐ before upgrade ■ after upgrade

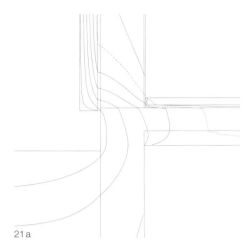

21a

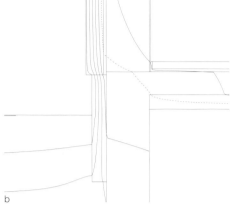

b

Energy Conservation Act requirements:

Requirements to be satisfied by floors over unheated basements to which linings are attached to the soffit:

max. U-value 0.40 W/m²K

or where floor finishes are renewed:

max. U-Wert 0.50 W/m²K

The requirements of the Act are met when the maximum possible thickness of insulation is provided on top of the floor without raising the door lintel.

U-value calculation with insulation to soffit of floor over basement:

	d [m]	λ [W/mK]	1/Λ [m²K/W]
R_{se}			0.170
EPS insulation	0.060	0.035	1.714
Reinf. concrete slab	0.160	2.300	0.070
EPS insulation	0.020	0.040	0.500
Cement screed	0.045	1.400	0.032
Ceramic tiles	0.012	1.300	0.009
R_{si}			0.170
Total thermal resistance			2.665
U-value [W/m²K]			**0.38**

U-value calculation with insulation to top of floor over basement:

	d [m]	λ [W/mK]	1/Λ [m²K/W]
R_{se}			0.170
Reinf. concrete slab	0.160	2.300	0.070
Vacuum ins. panel	0.020	0.004	5.000
Underfloor heating	0.020	0.320	0.063
Granite floor tiles	0.020	2.800	0.007
R_{si}			0.170
Total thermal resistance			5.479
U-value [W/m²K]			**0.18**

21 Isotherms for external wall with thermal insulation composite system without (a) and with (b) perimeter insulation for standard conditions to DIN 4108-2 (-5°C outside temperature, +20°C room temperature, 50% internal r.h.)
——— 9.3°C isotherm (risk of condensation)
········ 12.6°C isotherm (risk of mould growth)
22 Heat losses and heating energy requirement in kWh/a before and after upgrading:
losses through floor over basement with soffit insulation and via thermal bridges over the entire building (thermal bridge heat-loss coefficient reduced from 0.10 to 0.05 W/m²K because balcony slab cut off flush with masonry).

Perimeter insulation
Floor insulation on the cold or warm side

The majority of existing buildings have a reinforced concrete ground floor and uninsulated base over an unheated basement. Both act as particularly effective thermal bridges once a thermal insulation composite system has been installed. In this case the solid part of the external wall is located in the warm zone and therefore leads to a considerably higher heat loss through the base. The base should therefore always be insulated as well in the case of new external insulation even though these insulation measures are not explicitly required by the Energy Conservation Act. Furthermore, perimeter insulation may also be sensible as an individual measure on older buildings to combat mould growth in this zone in ground-floor apartments. However, sheet metal is the only way to protect such insulation against the rigours of the weather.

Costs normally dictate that the floor over an unheated basement be insulated on the underside (cold side). The prerequisite is, however, that the ceiling height in the basement permits such insulation in the first place and that services attached to the soffit do not present any major problems. Insulation to the top (warm) side of the floor over the basement is a rarity. Such a solution requires completely new floor finishes on the ground floor. However, such an approach is justified when the heating system is to be changed to underfloor heating at the same time. This usually results in deeper floor finishes, which reduce the clear heights beneath door and window lintels. The variation illustrated at the bottom of p. 45 is possible thanks to modern building materials technology and results in a minimal additional floor thickness. Nevertheless, it is an economic solution.

□ a
Continue the perimeter insulation at least 500 mm below the soffit of the ground floor slab when the basement is unheated. As the ground floor slab is usually at a much higher level than the surrounding ground, the earthworks for this are not usually particularly costly. Use non-absorbent, water-resistant materials for the insulation below ground and in the splashing water zone. Certain types of insulating systems may preclude the need for additional waterproofing of the base zone. Follow the instructions of the system manufacturer.

□ b
The junction between facade and plinth insulation can either be emphasized through an offset in the finishes or played down in the seamless option – merely a change in the insulating materials.
An offset as shown here requires the bottom edge of the thermal insulation composite system to be finished off with a trimming member to protect the front edge against mechanical damage. Aluminium sections can be used, on which the insulating boards are supported, or, as in this example, special systems with a thermal break where a rigid insulating block is punctured by a sheet-metal angle.

□ c
In the simplest case, simply glue the insulating material to the soffit of the ground floor slab; additional mechanical fixings or ceiling finishes are not essential. It is always advisable to employ soffit insulation in conjunction with external perimeter insulation. Once soffit insulation has been attached, the entire floor over the basement is on the warm side, which substantially increases the heat loss via an uninsulated plinth. Without perimeter insulation, there is no appreciable increase in the surface temperatures precisely at the

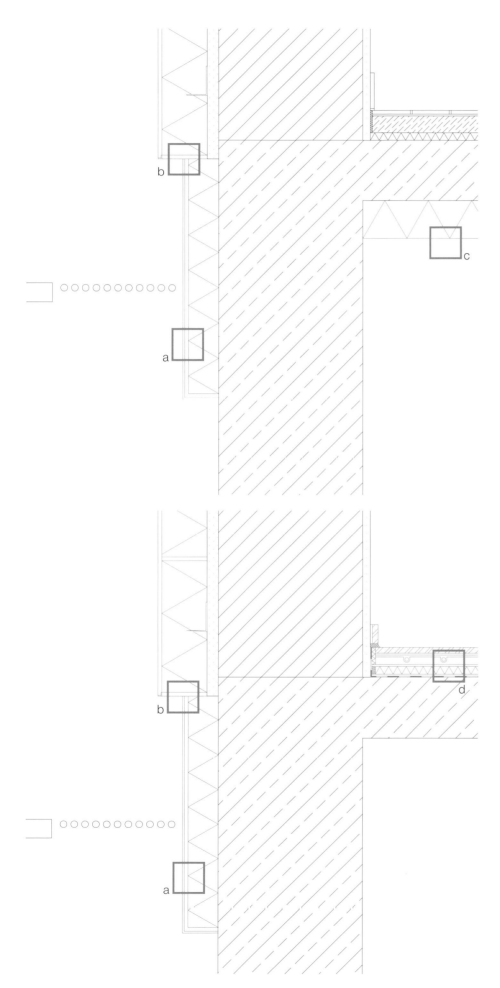

critical junction between internal floor finishes and external wall. Part of the reduced heat loss to the unheated basement is then cancelled out again by the enhanced thermal bridge losses in the plinth zone.

☐ d
Remove the old floor finishes first, down to the structural floor slab. The new floor finishes selected here consist of vacuum insulation panels (VIP) with 0.004 W/mK thermal conductance. What this means is that these 20 mm thick special insulating boards are equivalent to about 200 mm of conventional insulation. These sensitive vacuum insulation panels are protected against damage before and during installment by supplying them as rigid sandwich elements factory-customised to the sizes required. Lay an underfloor heating system (no screed: minimum thickness) on top.

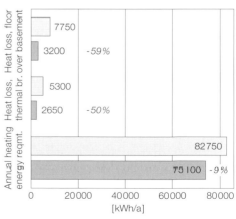

Heat loss, floor thermal br. over basement	7750			
	3200	*-59%*		
	5300			
	2650	*-50%*		
Annual heating energy reqmt.				82750
			75100	*-9%*

[kWh/a]

22 ☐ before upgrade ▨ after upgrade

45

1 Office building
   a elevation (before refurbishment)
   b plan
   c elevation (after refurbishment)

1a

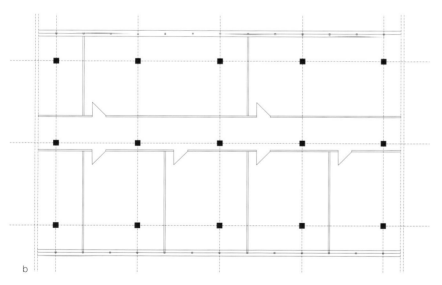

b

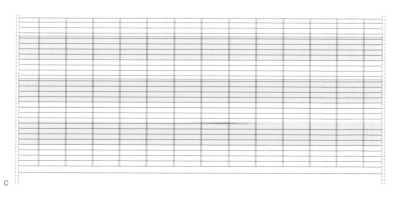

c

Upgrading the construction
Building B

Building B is a typical office block dating from the 1970s. In contrast to Building A, the solutions shown on the following pages are not individual upgrading measures for overcoming typical weaknesses, but instead represent a complete refurbishment concept to improve the energy performance. In this case the alterations to the fabric of the building go much further than is the case for Building A. All detail drawings have been drawn to a uniform scale of 1:10.

This is a three-storey office building with a reinforced concrete frame and two rows of offices with central corridor oriented east-west. The basement is set back on the line of the columns (see figure 4, p. 49) and is unheated. The facade consists of precast concrete elements for the spandrel panels and aluminium windows with fixed glazing. Apart from the reflective solar-control glass, there are no further sunshading measures. The interior is heated and cooled via induction units fitted in front of the spandrel panels. An oil-fired boiler provides the necessary heating energy, the cooling units are electric.

There have been no major changes to the building since it was first erected. Only the air-conditioning plant in the basement was replaced by a more modern installation around 1985. As the building is in need of refurbishment, the comfort expectations of the staff have risen in the meantime, and the cost of energy is constantly on the increase, an energy-efficiency upgrade is planned.

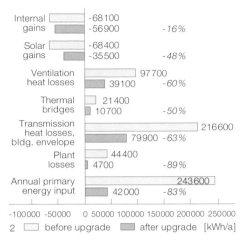

-100000 -50000 0 50000 100000 150000 200000 250000

2 ☐ before upgrade ▉ after upgrade [kWh/a]

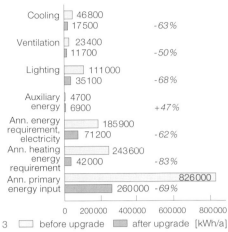

0   200000   400000   600000   800000

3 ☐ before upgrade ▉ after upgrade [kWh/a]

U-values of existing building

External wall:

	d [m]	λ [W/mK]	1/Λ [m²K/W]
R_{se}			0.040
Precast concrete	0.080	2.100	0.038
Mineral fibre	0.040	0.040	1.000
Reinforced concrete	0.200	2.100	0.095
R_{si}			0.130
Total thermal resistance			1.303
U-value of external wall [W/m²K]			**0.77**

Flat roof:

	d [m]	λ [W/mK]	1/Λ [m²K/W]
R_{se}			0.040
Roof waterproofing	0.008	0.170	0.047
Rigid PS foam	0.050	0.040	1.250
Vapour barrier	0.005	0.170	0.029
Reinforced concrete	0.240	2.100	0.114
R_{si}			0.100
Total thermal resistance			1.580
U-value of flat roof [W/m²K]			**0.63**

Floor over basement:

	d [m]	λ [W/mK]	1/Λ [m²K/W]
R_{se}			0.170
Reinforced concrete	0.240	2.100	0.114
Rigid PS foam	0.020	0.040	0.500
Cement screed	0.050	1.400	0.036
R_{si}			0.170
Total thermal resistance			0.990
U-value of floor over basement [W/m²K]			**1.01**

Existing situation

The German Energy Agency values (see p. 24) cannot be used for Building B because those values apply to residential buildings only. It is therefore necessary to calculate the U-values separately, which results in the following values for Building B:

- external wall   0.77 W/m²K
- windows   2.80 W/m²K
- flat roof   0.63 W/m²K
- floor over basement   1.01 W/m²K

In non-residential buildings the energy parameters according to draft standard DIN V 18599 do not refer to the useable floor space of the Energy Conservation Act, but instead pertain always to the actual net floor area. The assumptions made here result in an annual heating energy requirement of approx. 95 kWh/m²a. For simplicity, the entire heating installation is again assumed to have a degree of efficiency of approx. 70%, which translates into an annual heating oil consumption of approx. 14 l/m³ of heated building volume.
However, cooling, ventilating and lighting the building consumes even more energy, which must be provided by electricity – amounting to approx. 100 kWh/m²a. The electricity requirements can be broken down as follows:

- cooling   26 kWh/m²a
- ventilation   13 kWh/m²a
- lighting   61 kWh/m²a

If we consider the losses in the provision of this energy as well, this results in a primary energy input for the entire building of almost exactly 460 kWh/m²a.

Analysis

The heating costs in winter are too high. This is due to:

- high transmission heat losses through the building envelope
- high ventilation heat losses through the excessive air change rates of the ventilation system

Despite the cooling system (with its high energy input), the interior temperatures in summer are still too high. This is due to:

- lack of or inadequate sunshading
- poor glazing with excessive total energy transmittance (g-value)
- high internal heat gains through lighting and IT equipment
- no effective heat storage mass (reinforced concrete floors and spandrel panels are separated from the interior climate by suspended ceilings, linings and carpeting)

The lighting fittings consume too much electricity. This is due to:

- poor glazing with inadequate daylight transmittance (τ-value)
- poor interior design (dark, low-reflection surfaces)

Upgrading concept

Minimise the transmission heat losses via the building envelope:

- Remove precast concrete elements from facade, reduce height of spandrel panels, reduce insulation in external wall.
- Install new windows.
- Build transparent outer leaf in front of facade.
- Add additional insulation on top of flat roof.
- Add insulation to soffit of floor over basement.

2 Heat gains, heat losses and heating energy requirements in kWh/a before and after upgrading.
   The savings due to the night-time reductions are
   taken into account in the plant losses.
3 Electricity requirements for cooling, ventilation,
   lighting and auxiliary energy for heating plant,
   plus final energy requirement and primary energy
   input before and after upgrading.
4 Section through facade (before refurbishment)

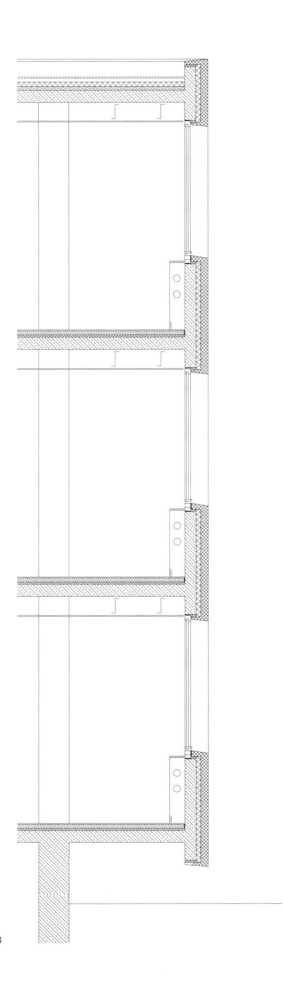

4

Reduce heat gains:
· Install temporary sunshades.
· Install glass with a low g-value.
· Convert to energy-saving IT equipment
  (e.g. replace CRT monitors by LCD
  monitors).
· Lower artificial lighting requirement.

Activate existing, and if necessary, fit
new, heat storage mass:
· Expose or ventilate reinforced concrete
  components.
· Install latent storage mass made from
  phase-change materials (PCM).
· Create natural ventilation options (primarily at night).

Improve the use of daylight:
· Increase the size of the windows.
· Install glass with high τ-value.
· Install reflective ceiling surfaces.
· Use sunshades (aluminium louvres) to
  direct the light.

Improve the lighting installation:
· Install efficient lighting fittings (electronic ballasts, daylight-based controls,
  movement detectors).
· Illuminate the rooms according to
  requirements (zoning of illumination levels).

Following the refurbishment and upgrading measures, the primary energy input is
only approx. 144 kWh/m²a. Just 23 kWh/
m²a of this is for heating, which with
improved plant leads to an annual heating oil consumption of approx. 3.3 l/m³ of
heated building volume. And the electricity consumption is now 36 kWh/m²a, broken down as follows:
· cooling   10 kWh/m²a
· ventilation   7 kWh/m²a
· lighting   19 kWh/m²a

An analysis of the summertime thermal performance according to DIN 4108-2 (Jul 2003) must be carried out if the proportion of window area related to the net floor area of the critical room or zone under consideration is > 10% for south-, east- or west-facing walls, or > 15% for north-facing walls. The analysis requires two values to be determined and then compared:

Solar gain index S

$$S = \frac{(A_w \cdot g_{total})}{A_g}$$

A_w = area of windows [m^2]
g_{total} = total energy transmittance of glass including, sunshading, calculated from gtotal
$g_{total} = g \cdot F_c$.
guaranteed manufacturer's information may be used
A_g = net floor area of room or part of room

Permissible maximum value S$_{perm}$

The permissible maximum value is a factor of the location of the building, the type of construction, the options for increased night-time ventilation, the type of glazing and the inclination and orientation of glazed surfaces.
Each of the six aforementioned criteria is attributed a proportional solar gain index according to a specific method. Added together, they give the permissible maximum value.

Evaluation

If the solar gain index S is less than the permissible maximum value S$_{perm}$, the summertime minimum thermal performance criterion has been met.

The analysis of the summertime thermal performance according to the Energy Conservation Act is based on the same calculation. However, in contrast to the minimum thermal performance, this analysis is only necessary if the total window area related to the total area of the facade is > 30%. According to the Act, roof surfaces also count towards the area of the facade when heated rooms are located directly below these surfaces.

The requirement for analysing the summertime minimum thermal performance is therefore more stringent in DIN 4108-2 than in the Energy Conservation Act. This means that an analysis of the summertime minimum thermal performance according to DIN 4108-2 automatically complies with the Act.

Facade

One of the biggest problems in existing non-residential buildings is the severe temperature rise inside the building during the summer. This drop in the level of comfort is either simply accepted or the rooms are cooled with a mechanical system, which leads to an increase in energy consumption. One of the primary aims of upgrading a non-residential building is therefore improving the summertime thermal performance.

☐ a
Adding a functioning sunshading system to the building is one of the most efficient ways of reducing the thermal loads in summer. DIN 4108-2 (Jul 2003), table 8, uses the factor Fc to classify sunshading according to its solar radiation permeability as follows:
· no sunshade, $F_c = 1$
· internal sunshade, $F_c = 0.75–0.9$
· external sunshade, $F_c = 0.25–0.5$

☐ b
Optimising the glass itself is very important. In non-residential buildings, reducing the solar radiation transmittance – represented by the total energy transmittance (g-value) – combined with a high daylight utilisation is more important than thermal performance. The so-called selectivity of the glass, expressed as the quotient of τ-value and g-value, should be > 2 for glass optimised for the summer. Such optimised glass types have, for example, a U-value of 1.0 W/m^{2}K, a g-value of 30% and a τ-value of 64%. The product of F_c value and g-value is the g_{total} value, which is the critical figure for the solar energy gain.

☐ c
A double facade with an outer skin of single glazing is a good solution – especially for refurbishment work – when constructional

or sound insulation problems must be considered as well as energy performance issues. The second skin protects existing concrete facades against the rigours of the weather, improves the sound insulation and as it is weatherproof and intruder-proof also allows the building to be ventilated at night. It also improves the thermal performance of the facade so that further insulating measures can be reduced.
In a double facade, half of the facade area should have opening lights or vents to avoid overheating the cavity. Glass-louvre facades are ideal for this application.

☐ d
In the absence of storage masses, heat gains warm up a room very quickly and lead to overheating. The excess thermal energy must then be dissipated by mechanical cooling systems. Storage masses, e.g. concrete floor slabs, are able to absorb large quantities of heat without heating up too much themselves. The greater the quantity of heat leading to a temperature rise of 1 K, the more effective the storage mass is. Storage masses can be activated up to a thickness of 100 mm. With 60 Wh thermal energy, a 100 mm thick concrete component heats up by 1 K/m^2. The storage capacity of a timber floor of equal thickness is only one-third of this – thermal energy equivalent to 20 Wh leads to the same temperature rise.

The lower temperature of the night-time air can be exploited to dissipate the heat stored during the day, provided reliable ventilation is possible during the night. Storage mass must therefore be exposed so that its effectiveness, as described above, can be activated.
If this is not possible because of other requirements (sound insulation, building

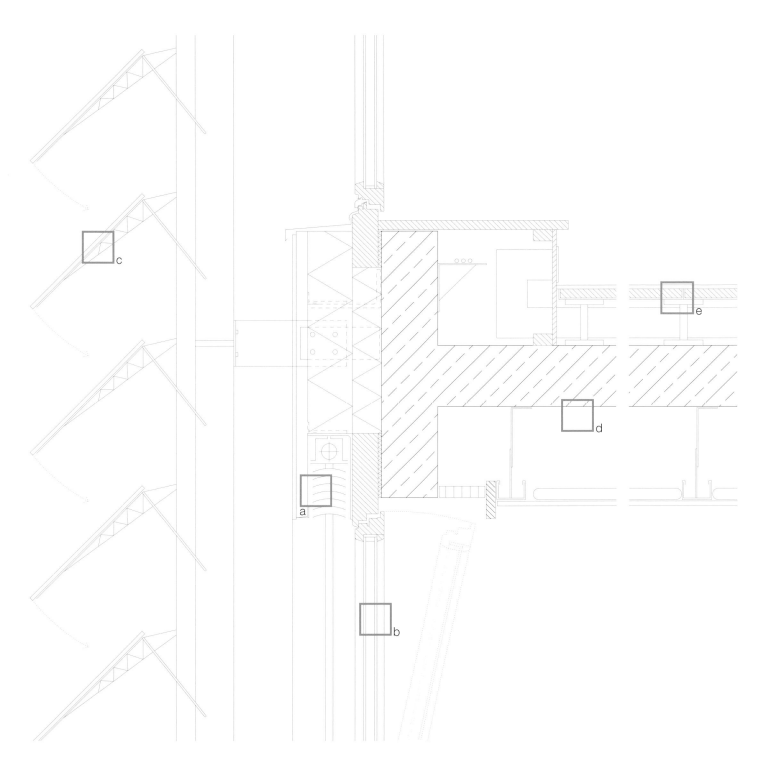

services), storage mass can also be retrofitted. By installing 20–40 mm thick latent
storage panels made from phase-change
materials, which at an air temperature of
25°C change from the solid to the liquid
state, a storage mass comparable to that
of a concrete floor slab can be achieved.
In the example shown here, the cool night-
time air is blown by a fan through the cavity between the suspended ceiling and
the reinforced concrete floor slab so that
the heat storage components can be
directly cooled.

□ e

Non-residential buildings must satisfy
high demands with regard to the flexibility
of their plan layouts. One primary requirement here is being able to retrofit or mod-
ify building services easily. Refurbishing
floor finishes, for instance, is fascilitated
by a raised or access floor. Such a floor
can accommodate electric cables plus
heating, cooling and ventilation ducts/
pipes in such a way that access to the
systems is possible at all times.

Energy Conservation Act requirements:

Requirements to be satisfied by a flat roof after upgrading:

max. U-value: 0.25 W/m²K

When tapering insulation is used, determine the U-value according to DIN EN ISO 6946, appendix C. The minimum thermal performance to DIN 4108-2 with a U-value of 0.75 W/m²K must also be guaranteed at the lowest point with the smallest thickness of insulation.

Correction factor for upside-down roofs

In an upside-down roof, it is essential to consider the additional heat losses due to precipitation water that passes through the joints between the insulation and drains away on the roof waterproofing. DIN 4108-2 and DIN EN ISO 6946, appendix D, cover this correction factor. It depends on the average amount of precipitation during the heating period, the watertightness of the joints between the insulation and the insulation properties of the roof finishes below the waterproofing. It is normally prescribed in the building authority approval documents for each individual insulating material.

The DIN 4108-2 correction factor for extruded PS foam boards with a peripheral rebate is as follows:

Proportion of thermal resistance R on room side of waterproofing compared to total thermal resistance [%]	Increase in U-value [W/m²K]
< 10 %	0.05
≥ 10 % to ≤ 50 %	0.03
> 50 %	0.00

U-value calculation:

Flat roof:	d [m]	λ [W/mK]	1/Λ [m²K/W]
R_{se}			0.040
Extruded PS foam	0.120	0.035	3.529
Waterproofing	0.008	0.170	0.047
Rigid PS foam	0.050	0.040	1.250
Vapour barrier	0.005	0.170	0.029
Reinforced concrete	0.240	2.100	0.114
R_{si}			0.100
Total thermal resistance R			5.109
U-value of flat roof [W/m²K]			**0.20**

U-value of flat roof [W/m²K]	0.20
Corr. factor (proportion$_R$ = 31 %) [W/m²K]	0,03
U-value of upside-down roof [W/m²K]	**0.23**

Flat roof

The most stringent requirements of the Energy Conservation Act apply to the refurbishment of flat roofs because this is where relatively low-cost insulation measures can be employed to realise a high energy-saving potential.

In the case of an existing warm deck design (flat roof with no ventilation cavity), the first step before refurbishment is to establish whether the flat roof finishes are intact, and merely an energy-efficiency upgrade is required, or whether all the finishes including waterproofing must be renewed.

In the case of an existing cold deck design (flat roof with ventilation cavity), the ventilation cavity is not usually deep enough to accommodate additional insulating material and still reliably satisfy the ventilation requirements. An analysis of the existing roof finishes is required to establish whether the building performance characteristics of the roof are still satisfactory if the ventilation cavity is filled completely with insulating material. If this is so, the roof can be refurbished extremely cost-effectively by blowing cellulose flakes into the cavity. Otherwise, the roof finishes including waterproofing must be renewed completely.

☐ a
If the roof waterproofing of a warm deck is intact, it is possible to add further insulation on top of the existing waterproofing. Use a closed-pore material, e.g. XPS, preferably with rabbet edges. This creates a so-called upside-down roof, which presents no building performance problems. The additional insulation protects the roof waterproofing against mechanical damage and also reduces the effect of temperature fluctuations. The actual drainage level is now on top of the new insulation, which requires gravel as ballast to prevent uplift.

☐ b
It may be necessary to raise the height of the parapet in order to accommodate the thicker roof assembly. The reference level for the height of the parapet is in this case the top of the layer of gravel.

☐ c
To avoid thermal-bridge losses, it is essential to insulate both sides of a concrete parapet and also the top if the height dictates this. Insulation of the inside of the parapet is often missing on older buildings.

☐ d
Renewal of the waterproofing is always necessary on cold decks or warm decks with defective waterproofing, but cheaper insulating materials (EPS or mineral wool) can be used for the additional insulation beneath the new waterproofing. It may be possible to leave the old roof finishes in place, but this depends on the materials used and their building performance properties. Whereas the bituminous waterproofing materials used almost exclusively in the past were very vapour-tight, the synthetic materials available these days are to a certain degree open to diffusion. This fact means that saturated roof finishes can gradually dry out again after the refurbishment work is complete. Leaving the existing roof finishes in place saves the cost of removal and disposal, and once they are dry again they help contribute to the thermal insulation.

☐ e
Owing to its mass, the addition of rooftop planting to a refurbished flat roof evens out temperature fluctuations and hence improves the summertime thermal performance of the building. At the same time, the roof waterproofing is protected against excessive thermal fluctuations,

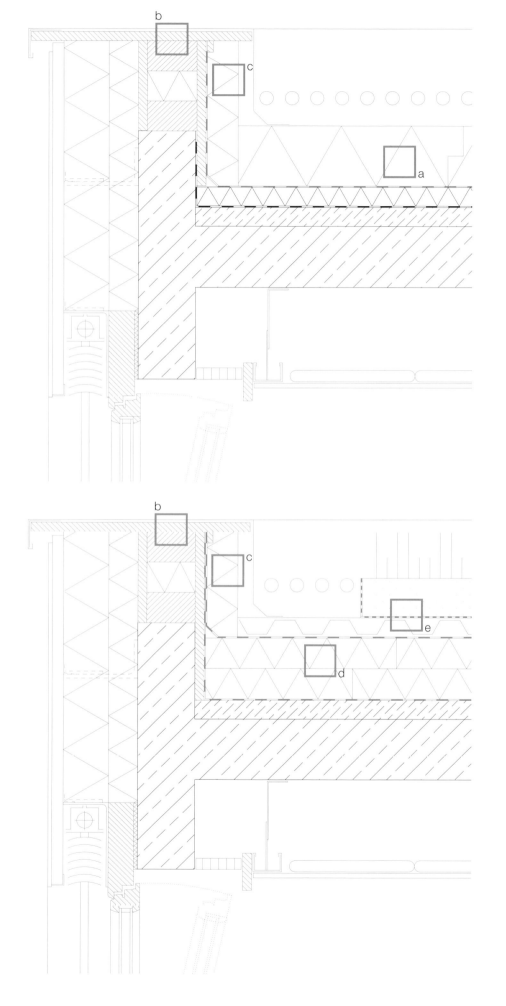

which may extend its useful life. It is essential to clarify in advance whether the roof slab can carry the additional loads. We distinguish between two types of rooftop planting:

· Intensive
  This is a two-level design with drainage, filter and plant-bearing layers.
· Extensive
  This is a single-level design without drainage layer but with a water-permeable plant-bearing layer and exclusively low-maintenance sedum varieties.

Intensive rooftop planting is also possible on flat roofs without falls provided an adequately deep drainage layer is included. And if a screed or insulation laid to falls is not necessary, then this cuts the cost of refurbishment. However, excessive roof falls tend to have a negative effect on the water balance of the plant-bearing layer. The weight of the lightest extensive rooftop planting designs is < 100 kg/m^2 in the saturated condition, and they add no more than 90 mm to the thickness of the roof finishes. However, owing to the lack of a drainage layer, such a minimal design requires a 2% fall.

Besides the constructional and thermal advantages, rooftop planting fulfils important ecological functions, particularly in urban environments.

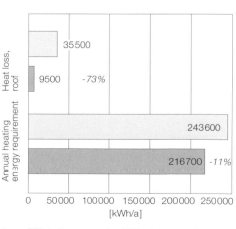

5   ☐ before upgrade   ▨ after upgrade

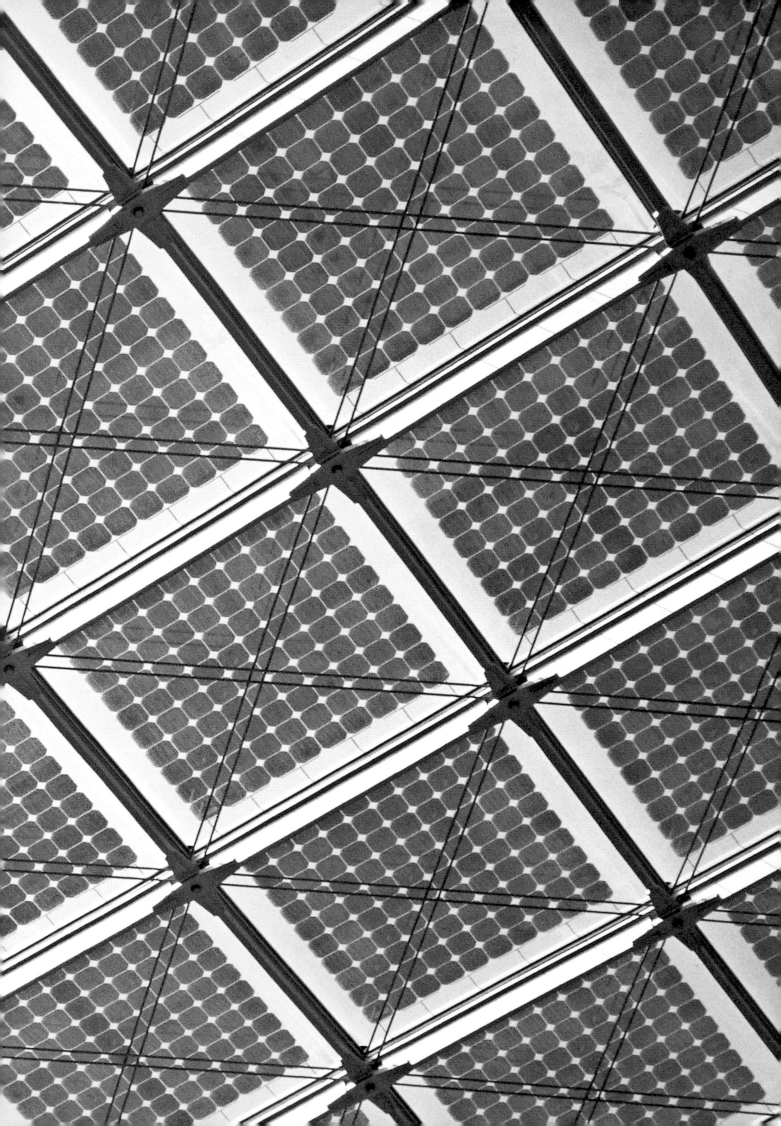

Upgrading the installations

The energy and resources consumed in
the conditioning of internal spaces are
influenced, on the one hand, by the constructional concept and, on the other, by
the nature and efficiency of the plant,
installations and systems. Since the EU
directive on the energy performance of
buildings came into force, we now have,
for the first time, a means of measuring
the total energy-related costs in connection with the use of a building.
Whereas in the past only the heating
requirements were considered, today all
factors of conditioning are taken into
account. Besides the energy input for the
heating, the energy input for cooling, ventilation and lighting are also considered
and evaluated by means of defined variables.
However, the principle still applies that,
essentially, a building should be able to
regulate the climatic fluctuations during
summer and winter itself. So, more than
ever before, architects are called upon to
develop building concepts that have a
low heating energy requirement, do not
overheat in summer, are provided with
optimum levels of daylight and can be
ventilated naturally. Only in this way can
we create the framework necessary to
ensure that the remaining conditioning
requirements can be met with efficient
installations which include the use of
renewable energy sources.

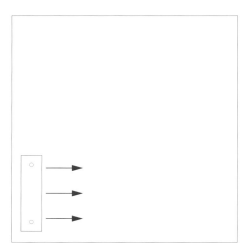

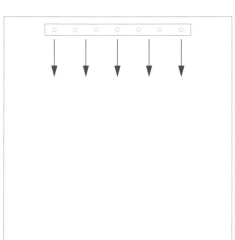

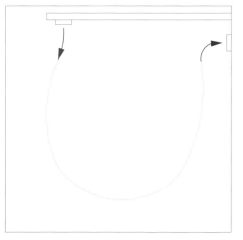

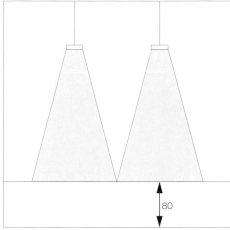

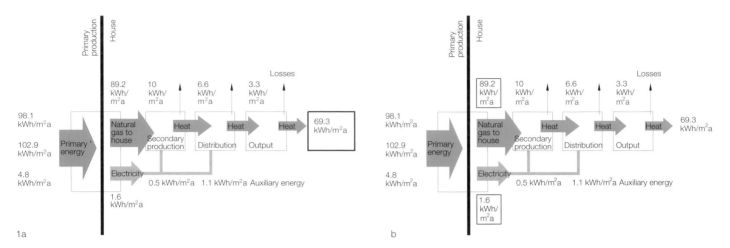

1a   b

The environmental relevance of installations can be assessed by means of the primary energy requirement and the carbon dioxide (CO_2) emissions. However, the statutory methods only make use of the primary energy assessment.
The assessment of the primary energy requirement is always based on the available energy requirement, e.g. the amount of heat that must be fed into a building in order to achieve the desired room temperatures (available energy, heating, see figures 1a-1d), or to cover the hot-water requirements. The amount of heat required is provided by the heating plant, conveyed to the rooms and output there at the places required via controllable devices. The heat losses that ensue during this process, which differ according to the degree of efficiency of the installation, are added to the available energy, which results in the figures for "final energy requirement, space heating" or "final energy requirement, hot water". In addition, the final energy requirement for electricity is also assessed because it is required as an auxiliary energy source for distributing the energy within the building (e.g. electricity for pumps and fans). In order to be able to assess these final energy requirements with regard to their relevance in environmental terms, they are multiplied by a primary energy factor according to DIN 4701-10 (figure 2) depending on the type of energy used. The primary energy factor fp corrects the final energy requirement so that it takes account of the consumption of resources required for the production and transport of the energy to the building. Besides objectively calculated data, the political aspects of the respective energy source also play a role here. In Germany electricity carries a particularly high primary energy factor because the mixture of energy sources is assumed to include 50% generated in coal-fired power sta-

tions with their high consumption of resources, since (with current technologies) two-thirds of the potential energy contained in the fuel is lost.

District heating systems, which – through a combined heat and power (CHP) arrangement – exploit the waste heat of steam turbines generating electricity, has a good primary energy factor. The use of renewable fuels is also very favourably assessed.

Using the primary energy as the parameter for the environmental compatibility of the installations in buildings involves a very abstract value which calls for some background information. Furthermore, due to the term itself and its unit of measurement (kWh), confusion with "true" energy quantities such as heating energy requirement or heating energy consumption cannot be ruled out. In particular, the end user may be led astray, and may not be fully aware of the actual heating costs of a property heated with, for example, district heating, which, as mentioned, has a good primary energy factor.
Nevertheless, the statutory methods of assessment use exclusively the primary energy for the energy-related assessment of buildings.

Much more transparent in this respect is the CO_2 parameter, which reveals at first glance that it is the environmental relevance of the technology installed that is being assessed, i.e. the actual, resulting emissions of pollutants.
Carbon dioxide causes changes in the enclosing layer of air that surrounds the Earth and separates it from outer space. Short-wave solar radiation can penetrate this layer, but as the content of CO_2 in the atmosphere rises, the latter retains more and more of the long-wave radiation reflected from the Earth. In the medium-

term, therefore, a temperature rise in the Earth's atmosphere is unavoidable. The level of greenhouse gas (GHG) emissions is measured in terms of CO_2 equivalent (CO_2 eq), which is linked with the use of an energy source. The GHG emissions are determined according to "GEMIS" (Global Emissions Model of Integrated Systems), which was first devised in 1987 by the Freiburg-based Institute for Applied Ecology and the University of Kassel and since then has been continually upgraded. The CO_2 parameter (CO_2 eq GHG emissions, figure 2) defined for each energy source includes all the pollutants that lead to environmental contamination, like CO_2 itself. As with the primary energy factor, this parameter also includes all the aspects relevant to the production and transport of the energy.

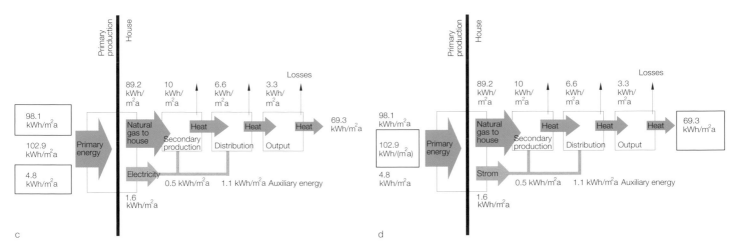

c   d

1   The calculation of the primary energy requirement for the heating is shown here using the example of a detached house.

a 1st step

Calculation of the available energy requirement, i.e. in this case the energy requirement due to the constructional concept (69.3 kWh/m²a). This is made up of
- transmission heat losses,
- ventilation heat losses,
- solar gains, and
- internal gains.

b 2nd step

Calculation of the final energy requirement, i.e. the quantity of energy that must be supplied to the house (89.2 kWh/m2a). Besides the heating energy requirement, this includes the following installation losses:
- production losses,
- storage losses (no storage in this example),
- distribution losses, and
- transfer losses.

Although not required for providing the available energy (electricity for pumps and fans), the auxiliary energy requirement (1.6 kWh/m²a) is assessed at the same time.

c 3rd step

Evaluation of the final energy requirement for heating by multiplying the energy source used (gas in this example) by the primary energy factor according to DIN 4107-10 (98.1 kWh/m²a). The auxiliary energy is assessed similarly (4.8 kWh/m²a).

d 4th step

Assessment of the primary energy by adding together the primary energy figures for heating and auxiliary energy (102.9 kWh/m2a). The installation itself can be assessed in primary energy terms by using the plant cost index e_P, which is the quotient of primary energy and available energy, i.e. in this example
$e_P = 102.9/69.3 = 1.48$.

2   The production and use of energy sources is always linked with CO_2 emissions (exception: renewable energies and electricity from nuclear power).

The table shows parameters that describe the environmental relevance of an energy source:
- The CO_2 equivalent GHG (greenhouse gases) emissions assesses all the pollutant emissions associated with the energy source, converted to the CO_2 emissions per kilowatt-hour of final energy.
- The net calorific value specifies the energy content of the respective fuel itself.
- The energy content of a fuel can be better exploited by using the heat of the exhaust gases. If this energy gain is added to the net calorific value, we obtain the gross calorific value.
- The primary energy factor is basically identical to the CO_2 value, but expressed in a much more abstract form. In assessing the energy sources, there are minor differences, e.g. between gas and oil.

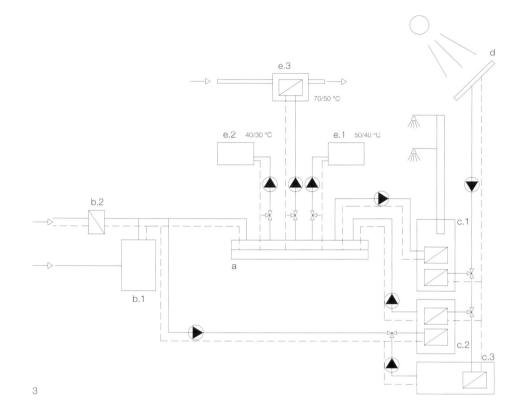

3   Schematic diagram of installation
    a Distribution manifold
    b Heat production
       b.1 Heating plant
       b.2 District heating input
    c Storage
       c.1 Hot-water tank
       c.2 Buffer tank
       c.3 Seasonal storage
    d Solar collector
    e Heat output
       e.1 High-temperature circuit (radiator)
       e.2 Low-temperature circuit (radiant panel)
       e.3 Warm-air heating

3

Heating installation

Buildings that are not connected to a group or district heating network usually have their own systems for providing heat. If the building is connected to a district heating system, the heating plant is replaced by a heat exchanger. In energy terms, district heating is a sensible solution, but owing to the high losses during distribution, is only viable within a radius of 5–10 km of the respective power station. The norm is, therefore, to install the heating plant in the building itself. A heating installation can be designed as a centralised or a decentralised system. In the former arrangement, a plant installed in the roof space has a number of advantages over a plant in the basement: a chimney is not required, and a solar energy system can be readily connected without the need for lengthy pipework. A decentralised system means that each apartment or housing unit has its own, local, separate installation. However, the integration of renewable energy sources is then inadvisable.

A heating installation is a closed circuit. Water is usually used as the heat transfer fluid, i.e. the means of transporting and storing the heat. The water is heated in a

boiler and, with the help of a pump, transported via pipes to the radiators. In installations requiring different temperatures, the distribution manifold, in combination with three-way mixing valves, ensures that the necessary quantity of hot water is fed into each heating circuit. The radiators emit the heat into the rooms. As the heat is emitted, the hot water cools and flows back via a return circuit to the boiler where it is heated again. Thermostats on the radiators or temperature sensors in the rooms regulate the heat output. External temperature sensors adjust the flow temperature to suit the momentary weather conditions. The flow and return temperatures differ depending on the type of heating system. In a typical oil- or gas-fired system with ribbed radiators, the flow temperature is 70°C and the return temperature 50°C; in a system with flat radiant panels, the temperatures are 35°C and 28°C respectively. In principle, heating installations with low system temperatures are more efficient and create a better internal climate.

Water tanks are often integrated into such systems to cover hot-water requirements and to act as a buffer for the heating system. Such buffer tanks reduce the cycle

frequency of non-modulating installations and hence improve the efficiency of the installation.

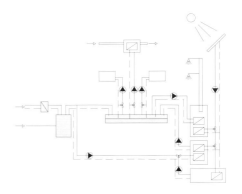

Heating plant

Combustion

Heat is normally produced by the direct combustion of raw materials, which are gas, oil and biomass. A modern odern oil- or gas-fired heating plant can modulate its heat output to suit the heating demands so that it is possible to produce the heat with minimal losses. A modulating method of operation is possible only to a limited extent when burning biomass (wood). A means of storing the heat is therefore required.

In group heating, one boiler supplies several buildings with heat. In district heating, whole communities or districts are supplied with heat from combined heat and power (CHP) plants by local power supply companies. Group or district heating networks are often supplemented by waste heat from electricity generation or waste incineration.

Low-temperature boiler

A low-temperature boiler adjusts its heat production automatically to suit the circumstances. The water is only heated to the temperature necessary to suit the external conditions. This is a prime reason for the higher degree of efficiency in modern low-temperature boilers compared to older models. However, they are also better insulated so that losses due to cooling are minimal.

Condensing boiler

Condensing boilers are more efficient than low-temperature boilers because they also use the heat from the flue gases, which pass through a heat exchanger to preheat the cold water in the return circuit. However, the cooled flue gases no longer possess sufficient thermal buoyancy and therefore must be helped with a fan (forced draught). Owing to the condensation and the overpressure in the flue-gas system, existing chimneys have to be upgraded to cope with condensing boilers. To do this, flues of glass or stainless steel, for example, are inserted into the old chimneys.

Electric heater

In an electric heater, electricity is converted directly into heat, and in the case of electric night-storage heaters it is stored in heat-retaining bricks. Owing to the great losses in the production and distribution of electricity, the overall degree of efficiency is very unfavourable. Electric heaters are sensible when the cost of producing heat with other systems is too high. For example, a solar energy system which heats the water but is assisted by electrical heating instead of having to fire up a boiler for a few hours in the summer.

Heat pump

It is possible to use a small amount of electrical energy to drive a compressor and then produce a considerably greater amount of heat energy by means of the thermodynamic cycle – the process used by a refrigerator. The outside air can be used as a heat source, but it is better to use the soil or the groundwater. Considering the high losses in electricity generation, the coefficient of performance (COP – the ratio of electricity used to heat energy obtained) should be at least 3. The smaller the rise in temperature from the heat source to the heating system flow temperature, the better is the COP.

Combined heat and power

The heart of a combined heat and power (CHP) plant is the engine or a gas turbine that drives an electric generator. The electricity generated is used in the building or fed into the mains network, while the waste heat is used for heating the building. Normally, a CHP plant covers the main loads in the heating period and an additional boiler cuts in to handle the peak loads. For economic reasons, CHP plants should only be used when heat is required and not just for generating electricity, and should be used throughout the year if at all possible. Ideally, CHP plants should be fully utilised in group heating networks with many users.

Fuel cell

In a fuel cell, hydrogen and oxygen, which are separated by an electrolyte, react with one another to form water. This process creates a stream of electrons and the fuel cell generates electricity. Like with CHP, the ensuing waste heat is used to heat the building. Hydrogen is not a true raw material because it first has to be produced, either from water by way of electrolysis, or by extracting it from natural gas. But hydrogen can be obtained without consuming resources if the electrolysis process is carried out using electricity from photovoltaic panels. It is possible to store the hydrogen generated by solar energy. However, fuel cell technology is still at the development stage.

4 Assessment of heating installation

The energy losses incurred during the production, distribution and output of the heat are known as the installation losses. The energy requirement of a building therefore results from the heating requirement and the installation losses. Due to their outdated heating plant technology, existing installations in particular achieve standard utilisation rates of 70%, i.e. 30% of the energy contained in the raw material is lost during the heat production. Poorly insulated horizontal and vertical distribution lines lead to further losses, which means that degrees of efficiency of 60% are quite realistic for existing installations. The first thing to do in every case is therefore to replace an existing, outdated installation by a new, more efficient installation, which can raise the overall degree of efficiency to 85%. For example, the generation of 10 000 kWh of available heat no longer requires 16 600 kWh of final energy (= 1660 l oil), but instead only 11 800 kWh (= 1180 l oil).

A new installation only reveals its full potential when, for example, the building's thermal insulation is also improved and the heating requirement is therefore reduced so that the installation can be operated with lower flow temperatures while retaining the existing radiators.

Energy efficiency evaluation – heating

		Degree of efficiency[1] [%]	Final[2] energy [kWh]	Resource	Primary energy [kWh]	CO_2 [kg]	Costs[3] [%]
1	**Low-temperature**						
1.1	Low-temperature (old)						
	Oil	70	14000	Oil	15400	4242	
	Gas	70	14000	Gas	15400	3486	
1.2	Low-temperature (new)						
	Oil	90	11000	Oil	12100	3333	100
	Gas	90	11000	Gas	12100		100
1.3	Wood pellets	80	12500	Wood	2500	525	200
2	**Gross calorific value**						
	Oil	95	10526	Oil	11600	3189	105
	Gas	98	10200	Gas	11220	2539	105
3	**Direct electricity**	100	10000	Electricity	30000	6470	120
4	**Heat pump**						
	Heat pump (electricity)	3.5–5[4]	2500		7500	1617	300
	Heat pump (gas)	3[4]	3300		3600	815	300
5	**Combined heat & power**						
5.1	Local CHP				4000	1578	200
	Heat production		20000	Oil	22000	6060	
	Electricity credit		6000		18000	4482	
5.2	Fuel cell[5]				1800	600	
	Heat production		18000	Gas	19800	4482	
	Electricity credit		6000		18000	3882	

Heating requirement of 10 000 kWh during heating period

[1] The standard utilisation rate describes the degree of efficiency of heat production under standardised conditions.
[2] Heating energy without auxiliary energy; the electricity supply is defined as heating energy in the case of heat pumps.
[3] Costs refer to the provision of heating plant without distribution and heat output.
[4] Alternative to standard utilisation rate: performance figure (ratio of heat energy produced [kWh] to electricity requirement [kWh]).
[5] Cost not available.

4

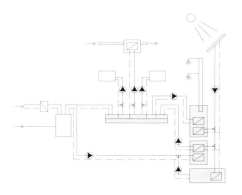

Heat storage

Storage media are used to separate the time of heat production and the time of heat utilisation.

We distinguish between long- and short-term storage media as well as between the types of storage. Sensible heat storage media change their temperature when absorbing or releasing thermal energy; in latent heat storage media, on the other hand, it is the state of the material used that changes. For example, water in its frozen state is a latent heat storage medium because it absorbs thermal energy upon melting without changing its temperature. After it has melted, it (now water) represents a sensible heat storage medium until the water boils. Water tanks are customarily used as short-term sensible heat storage media in space heating and hot-water systems. As a thermal stratification takes place in the storage medium, this effect should also be taken into account when introducing the thermal energy (top: hot; bottom: cold).

Hot-water storage

Only small amounts of water can be heated directly in instantaneous water heaters. Furthermore, solar energy cannot be used in such localised heating installations. Hot water is therefore held ready in tanks, the size of which is chosen to suit the number of occupants/users and their hot-water requirements.

Buffer tank

Buffer tanks in heating systems lead to a reduction in the cycle frequency in non-modulating heating plant. Buffer tanks are therefore always required when wood and other types of biomass are used for heating. A buffer tank is also advisable with heat pumps. The use of solar energy to boost heating requirements – in any type of heating installation – is only possible if the buffer tank is used as a "heat manager".

Seasonal storage

Seasonal storage enables the energy to be stored for a very long period, normally a whole season. Very large, highly insulated water tanks, latent heat storage media or the soil can be used. Ground couplings, e.g. heat sondes down to a depth of 100 m, should be considered not as energy sources, but rather as storage options, depending on regeneration ability and usage.

Seasonal storage can be used to store solar energy obtained efficiently in the summer to back up heating requirements significantly in winter.

Storage

Tank sizes (supply and install)		Reference size	Costs	Remarks
1	**Drinking water**			Figures are valid for 5 persons.
1.1	Drinking water (without solar)	60 l/person	2 €/l	
1.2	Drinking water (with solar)	80 l/person	3 €/l	
2	**Buffer storage (heating)**			The m² figure for reference size refers to the size of the collector.
2.1	Buffer storage (without solar)	10 l/kW	2 €/l	
2.2	Buffer storage (with solar)	50 l/m²	3 €/l	
3	**Long-term storage**			The m² figure for reference size refers to the size of the collector.
3.1	20 kWh/m²a heating backup	300 l/m²	0.20 €/l	
3.2	40 kWh/m²a heating backup	400 l/m²		
3.3	60 kWh/m²a heating backup	500 l/m²		

5   Solar energy can be stored in tanks for heating hot water, in combination tanks for boosting heating requirements and heating hot water, and in seasonal storage media for backing up the heating.

As seasonal storage is usually designed for several buildings together, the distribution losses are relatively high by the time the energy reaches the end user. It is therefore not recommended to heat the hot water in summer (when the heating is off) using the seasonal storage system.

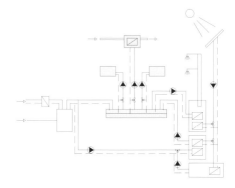

Heat output

Radiators
In existing buildings, convectors, ribbed radiators and flat radiant panels are the most common methods of delivering the heat to the rooms. They emit heat partly by way of radiation and partly by way of convection, and their efficiency depends on their size and the temperature of the hot water. If only the heating plant is renewed during upgrading measures, the radiators must be enlarged if the intention is to reduce the flow temperature. But if additional insulation is being fitted at the same time, this reduces the heating requirements and so the radiators can be left unchanged despite a lower flow temperature.

Coil heating
This type of heating system covers a large area and is operated with a low flow temperature. It can be fitted under floors and in walls, and in rooms with sufficient headroom, in the ceiling as well. As the heated surfaces transfer the heat to the room evenly via gentle radiation, they create a very pleasant internal climate. However, there is a delay between receiving the heat and transferring it to the room, and so such systems are difficult to regulate. Coil heating systems are therefore primarily suited to permanently heated rooms where the conditions remain fairly constant. Changes to the interior layout or usage can be accommodated to only a limited extent. By contrast, in such circumstances it is easier to replace or reposition radiators or adjust the flow temperature accordingly.

As coil heating systems can only be operated with low flow temperatures, their use in refurbishment projects is only advisable when the heating requirement is reduced at the same time.

Warm-air system
The maximum temperature for air blown into a room is 45°C. As air has only a limited heat absorption capacity, high air change rates and large duct cross-sections are required to convey larger amounts of warm air. Basically, owing to the high transport energy and the plant required, the quantity of air should be limited to that necessary for hygiene purposes. For these reasons, warm-air systems are therefore only suitable for well-insulated buildings with very low heating requirements (max. 20 W/m²). However, warm-air systems have one big advantage for such applications: ventilation (which is necessary, or at least advisable) and heating can both be provided by just one system.

6 Air can transport only a small amount of heat, which means that warm-air heating systems are only advisable for buildings with a low heating requirement.
Radiators allow the heat required to be dissipated in the smallest area. The lower the flow temperature, the larger the area for the heat output must be. 6 FT = flow temperature; RT = return temperature

Parameters for heat output		Heat output	Costs	Remarks
1	**Radiators** FT/RT 70/55°C FT/RT 50/40°C	1000–3000 W/m² 500–1500 W/m²	200 €/m²	
2	**Underfloor heating** FT/RT 40/35°C (wood-block flooring) FT/RT 50/45°C	60 W/m² 90 W/m²	40 €/m²	Costs relate to pipework and distributor.
3	**Hot air** fresh air 45°C/single air change fresh air 45°C/double air change	20 W/m² 40 W/m²	100 €/m² 80 €/m²	Ventilation with heat recov. costs include pipework.

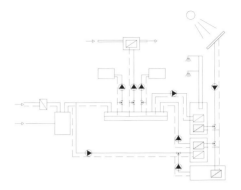

Solar heating systems

Every year, the radiation from the Sun that reaches the Earth is far more than we need. South-facing windows enable the solar radiation to be used passively to heat the interior. But when a solar heating system is used in conjunction with storage media, the solar energy can be used actively, i.e. irrespective of the building concept. In collectors, the solar energy heats up water-filled pipes which then feed a storage tank. Solar heating systems are primarily used for providing hot water. At today's energy prices, it is economically advisable to cover up to 70% of hot-water requirements with solar energy. Owing to the higher storage and control requirements, the use of solar energy to boost the space heating is not yet economic and therefore less frequently encountered in practice. However, a minimal backup for the heating system can be achieved relatively cheaply by adding a large buffer tank to the solar-powered hot-water system. This uses only the heat (generated by solar radiation) that builds up during the heating period, but more intensive use is possible with seasonal storage media.
Solar heating systems can also be relatively easily retrofitted to existing heating installations.

Flat-plate and tube collectors

The collectors form the heart of any solar heating system. They collect the solar radiation and heat up the water. A black absorbent material, usually with a selective coating, forms the surface of the collector. In a flat-plate collector, the absorber plates are fitted in a rectangular housing and covered with a pane of glass. In a vacuum-tube collector, the absorber plates are fitted within an evacuated glass tube. The vacuum ensures better insulation and hence improves the efficiency of the collector.

The absorber plates can be fitted within the collector housing to achieve an optimum heat gain even if the collector does not face south.

Air collectors

Air collectors work only in conjunction with a ventilation system. The external air is drawn in via a collector consisting of a system of round aluminium tubes fitted beneath a pane of glass. The air is thus heated up and can be supplied to the rooms directly or, if required, can be heated further in a heat exchanger working with the exhaust air.
If the heat is not required, it can be used to provide hot water via an air-to-water heat pump. Air collectors can also be used in conjunction with the adsorption method for building heating and cooling.

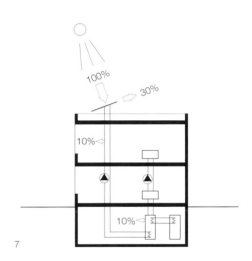

7

7   About 50% of the solar radiation incident on the collector can be used for heating hot water or boosting the space heating.
8   Incident solar radiation for Würzburg in southern Germany (Energy Conservation Act reference climate location) taken from DIN 4108-6 (Jun 2003). The upper figures in each line represent the average monthly solar radiation on surfaces at different angles. This figure has been multiplied by the number of hours in a month (e.g. 31 d x 24 h/d) to obtain the monthly energy quantity provided by the Sun (the lower figures in each line).

Incident solar radiation for Würzburg, Germany

Ref. climate, Germany		Average monthly radiation intensities [W/m²] and monthly energy quantities [kWh/m²]												Annual available solar rad. [kWh/m²]	Value for heating period [kWh/m²]
Orientation		Jan	Feb	Mar	Apr	May	Jun	Jul	Aug	Sep	Oct	Nov	Dec	Jan–Dec	Oct–Mar
Horizontal	0°	33	52	82	190	211	256	255	179	135	75	39	22	1120.0	225.0
		24.6	34.9	61.0	136.8	157.0	184.3	189.7	133.2	97.2	55.8	28.1	16.4		
South	30°	51	67	99	210	213	250	252	186	157	93	55	31	1216.0	295.0
		37.9	45.0	73.7	151.2	158.5	180.0	187.5	138.4	113.0	69.2	39.6	23.1		
	45°	57	71	101	205	200	231	235	178	157	97	59	34	1187.0	310.0
		42.4	47.7	75.1	147.0	140.0	100.3	174.8	132.4	113.0	72.2	42.5	25.3		
	60°	60	71	98	190	179	203	208	162	150	95	60	35	1104.0	310.0
		44.6	47.7	72.9	136.8	133.2	146.2	154.8	120.5	108.0	70.7	43.2	26.0		
	90°	56	61	80	137	119	130	135	112	115	81	54	33	810.0	270,0
		41.7	41.0	59.5	98.6	88.5	93.6	100.4	83.3	82.8	60.3	38.9	24.6		

8

Cooling installation

Depending on whether water or air is used as the heat transfer medium, a cooling installation consists of cooling surfaces or air outlets in the rooms, a chiller and a recooling unit. In the first step, heat is removed from the room through an exchange of air or a network of water-filled pipes. This process heats up the transfer medium which in turn transfers it to the refrigerant circulating in a chiller.

The refrigerant is heated further (above the temperature of the external air) so that the heat energy absorbed can be expelled to the outside air.
The transfer medium (refrigerant) can be heated by compression or by the direct addition of heat, depending on the type of chiller.
If heat is required for cooling, a solar or district heating system can be used for the heat production. Transferring the heat

to the soil or feeding it into the ground-water is also possible in the case of low cooling loads.
Chilling for a cooling installation can take place centrally for the whole building or locally using so-called multi-split appliances for individual groups of rooms. The cooling of individual rooms with separate equipment always leads to the problem of choosing the best position for the recooling unit (spoils the facade).

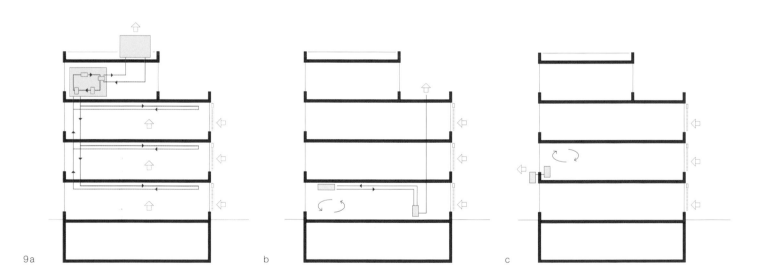

9a   b   c

Energy efficiency evaluation – cooling

		Final energy [kWh]	Resource/ aux. energy	Primary energy [kWh]	CO_2 emissions [kg]	Costs [%]	Remarks
1	Compression-type refrigeration unit (electricity)	5000	Electricity	15000	3235	120	Flexible in use
2	Compression type refrigeration unit (gas)	7000	Gas	7700	1743	140	Flexible in use
3	Absorption-type refrigeration unit	8000	Gas	8800	1992	180	Flexible in use
4	Adsorption-type refrigeration unit	8000	Gas	8800	1992	220	Only with air-conditioning
5	Soil[1]	1250	Electricity	3750	809	100	Only for low requirements
6	Groundwater[2]	1250	Electricity	3750	809	100	Only for low requirements
7	Night-time ventilation[3]	1200	Electricity	3600	776	100	Limited use

[1] Exchanger surfaces in the soil beneath the ground slab, which can be used for heating purposes in the winter.
[2] Wells down to a depth of approx. 5 m.
10 [3] Extra cost of larger installation where ventilation system exists already.

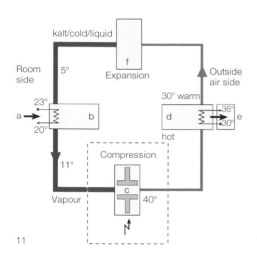

11

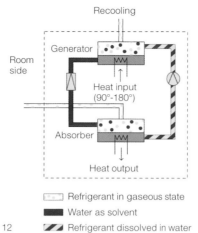

12

Legend
Refrigerant in gaseous state
Water as solvent
Refrigerant dissolved in water

13

Chiller plant

Compression-type refrigeration unit
To date, the thermodynamic cycle of the heat pump is the most common form of chiller plant. In the evaporator, i.e. on the cold side, there is a refrigerant at a low pressure which vaporises even at a low temperature. In doing so, it absorbs heat. An electrically driven pump is used to compress the vapour, which causes it to heat up further. The high temperature enables the heat to be dissipated to the outside air via the recooling unit. After that, the expansion valve allows the cooled refrigerant to expand in the evaporator and cool down again. The cycle begins anew.

Absorption-type refrigeration unit
The heat from the room is transferred to the refrigerant (ammonia), which thus starts to vaporise and is subsequently dissolved in water in the absorber. Part of the heat is released again here and can be used for the rest of the process. In the generator the refrigerant is boiled off from the water with a relatively small amount of heat. Thereafter, it is fed to the condenser, where it transfers its heat to the recooling circuit. The water returns to the absorber. The absorption heat pump requires considerably less power than the compression heat pump. However, the generator requires additional thermal energy, which, however, can be provided by solar power.

Adsorption-type refrigeration unit
Chilling through adsorption works only when cooling with fresh air and presumes the availability of a ventilation system. The thermodynamic process is, in principle, comparable with that of an air-conditioning installation (humidification, dehumidification, heating). However, there is no chilling with electricity, which is expensive in terms of primary energy and is necessary in a compression-type refrigeration unit. Instead, heat is used to initiate a physical process which exploits the fact that water cools when moisture is introduced and heats up when moisture is removed. The heat required can be provided by solar power.

9 a Cooling the whole building
   b Cooling storey by storey
   c Cooling individual rooms
10 Energy efficiency evaluation of different types of chiller plant for an assumed cooling requirement of 10 000 kWh during the summer.
11 Cooling with electricity:
   Compression-type refrigeration unit
   a Hot interior air or hot water
   b Water-to-refrigerant heat exchange (refrigerant vaporises)
   c Refrigerant heated by compression (electricity required)
   d Refrigerant-to-water heat exchange (hot water: recooling)
   e Recooling unit: water/outside air heat exchange
   f Expansion of refrigerant (return to liquid state and cooling)

12 Cooling with heat:
   Absorption-type refrigeration unit
   A thermal compressor (absorber + generator) is used instead of a compressor to raise the temperature of the refrigerant.
13 Cooling with heat:
   Adsorption-type refrigeration unit
   The temperatures in brackets are approximate values and serve to illustrate the process:
   a Fresh air for the interior (20°C/50% r.h.)
   b Exhaust air (26°C/70% r.h.)
   c Expelled air (32°C/80% r.h.)
   d Outside air (30°C/40% r.h.)
   e The exhaust air is humidified, which cools it (22°C/100% r.h.).
   f Heat recovery: the exhaust air removes heat from the hot outside air (cooling to 27°C/18% r.h.), which reduces the relative humidity of the exhaust air (41.5°C/32% r.h.).

g The exhaust air is further heated in a heater to reduce its relative humidity (to 49°C/22% r.h.).
h The relatively dry expelled air can absorb moisture from the outside air in the sorption wheel (or desiccant rotor) before it is released into the open air (expelled air: 32°C/80% r.h.). The removal of moisture from the outside air causes it to heat up (from 30°C/40% r.h. to 47°C/6% r.h.).
i The outside air cooled (to 27°C/18% r.h.) in the heat exchanger (f) is heated up with a heater (to 29°C/16% r.h.) so that it can subsequently be set to the desired internal temperature and relative humidity (20°C/50% r.h.) through precise humidification.

Cooling output

Cooling ceiling and component activation
Cooling elements can be attached directly to the soffit in the form of concealed pipes or suspended below in the form of panels. When the cooling elements form part of a ceiling system, then we speak of a cooling ceiling. If the cooling surfaces are suspended below the soffit as individual components, they are often referred to cooling fins. The cooling effect is essentially achieved by way of radiation and hence represents a very pleasant way of cooling. In all cooling installations it is important to make sure that no condensation forms, i.e. that the surface temperature of the cooling surfaces does not drop below the dew point temperature of the air in the room.
In the case of component activation, water pipes are laid in the soffit of a concrete floor slab. The direct contact between the cooling lines and the storage mass improves the storage effect. Despite relatively high flow temperatures, the large surface area in conjunction with the storage mass enables considerable heat loads to be dissipated because the system can be operated 24 hours a day. The high flow temperature also enables renewable energy sources such as geothermal heat or groundwater to be used efficiently.

Underfloor cooling
An underfloor heating system can be used for cooling in summer. This cuts the cost of separate heating and cooling systems. The cooling effect is achieved by direct contact and radiation. The disadvantage of underfloor cooling is that if the cooling effect is excessive, the thermal comfort of the occupants is severely impaired because the temperature difference between head and feet becomes too large. Underfloor cooling can therefore only be operated at a temperature only marginally different to that of the room. Its efficiency and applications are therefore limited.

Cold-air system
Cold-air cooling systems are found in either central or local fresh-air, recirculating-air or hybrid forms. In the recirculating-air system, the existing interior air is cooled, in the fresh-air variation, the air is drawn in from the outside. In a hybrid system, the warm exhaust air is mixed with the required amount of fresh air, cooled and then fed back into the room.
The cool incoming air can flow into the room at a high level, where natural thermal currents distribute it well around the room, or it can be blown in at high velocity at low level.
One especially hygienic and efficient form of supplying fresh air to the interior is through displacement ventilation. The cool fresh air gushes slowly through floor-level openings and forms a "sea" of cold air because it is heavier than the hot interior air. Internal heat sources such as people and equipment generate thermal currents and the air rises without the need for any mechanical assistance (fans).

14 Principles of cooling effects with water:
 a Cooling ceiling
 b Component activation (soffit)
 c Underfloor cooling
 with air:
 d Local recirculating cooling unit with central cold-air supply
 e Cold-air cooling with compact local unit
 f Central cold-air cooling
15 Performance data for different ways of achieving cooling

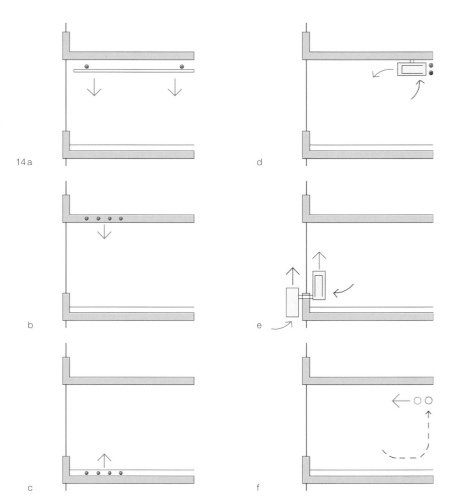

Performance data for different ways of achieving cooling

		Max. temp. difference[2]	max. output	Costs[1]	Remarks
1	**Cooling elements**				
1.1	Cooling ceiling[4]	8 K	100 W/m²	200–600 €/m²	[4] Cooling surface in conjunction with ceiling system
1.2	Cooling fins[5]	8 K	120 W/m²	400–800 €/m²	[5] Individual suspended panels
2	**Active storage[3]**				
2.1	Underfloor cooling	4 K	15–30 W/m²	0–40 €/m²	[3] Thermal storage activated
2.2	Concrete structure	4 K	40–60 W/m²	30–40 €/m²	by installation
3	**Air cooling**				
3.1	Single change of air	8 K	8 W/m²		Heating, cooling and ventilation
3.2	Double change of air	8 K	16 W/m²	300 €/m²	with one system
3.3	4-fold change of air	8 K	24 W/m²		

[1] The costs include neither chiller plant nor instrumentation and control.
[2] Temp. difference between interior air and cooling medium (risk of condensation, disrupted thermal comfort).

Regenerative cooling
If cooling is to be carried out without using any resources, simply the use of renewable energy sources, only small heat loads can be dissipated. Reducing the heat gains by means of constructional measures is therefore vital when deciding to use renewable energy for cooling.

Night-time ventilation
If storage masses are available and can absorb heat during the day, some of this heat can be released again through contact with the colder night air. However, one problem can be that windows left open at night are generally neither weatherproof nor intruder-proof. But if protected ventilation openings are available, natural ventilation can be boosted with the help of a low-power extract system.

Ground coupling
Thanks to its constant, moderate temperature over the whole year in depths down to 100 m, the soil offers an outstanding cold source. Underground heat exchangers for cooling the incoming air have been proving their worth for many years. Flat absorbers laid over a large area or sondes drilled deep into the ground enable water or a water/glycol mixture to be cooled down to temperatures of 12-16°C in the summer depending on capacity and depth of laying. Again, this cold source is best combined with a cooling system that activates storage masses. Owing to the large area required, this application is often problematic, particularly in refurbishment projects.

Groundwater
Groundwater can be used for cooling even more efficiently than the soil. The unceasing flow makes the heat absorption capacity of the groundwater almost infinite. In technical terms it is possible to install groundwater cooling even as part of the refurbishment project because the system requires little more than two wells – production and re-injection.

Recooling units
Recooling units are normally used to cool down the refrigerant in conventional refrigeration units. In the recooling circuit, the heat of the refrigerant is released into the environment using water as a medium. Recooling units are therefore always separate items located on the roof of a building. They can also be used for night-time cooling of cooling systems that activate storage masses, like the aforementioned concealed pipes of the cooling ceiling.

Solar-powered cooling
The absorption- and adsorption-type refrigeration units described on p. 65 can be operated with solar energy by ensuring that the process heat required comes from solar collectors.

Radiant cooling
One seldom-utilized regenerative cooling option makes use of the skyward radiation of the night sky in summer. One simple system uses swimming pool absorber mats mounted on the roof (flat or shallow-pitched roofs are best). The water circulating at night can cool the storage masses in the building directly or water in a tank. The average capacity of such a system in our latitudes is 50–80 W/m² of absorber surface.

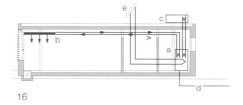

16

17

18

16 Solar cooling
  a Refrigeration unit (absorption or adsorption)
  b Cooling effect provided by fins or fresh air
  c Recooling
  d Electricity supply
  e Collector for producing heat
17 Ground coupling (groundwater)
  a Cooling effect provided by component cooling (floor/soffit)
  b Heat exchanger
  c Production and re-injection wells
18 Ground coupling (soil)
  a Cooling effect provided by component cooling (floor/soffit)
  b Heat exchanger
  c Absorber

Ventilation

In order to maintain hygienic air conditions, every room must be supplied with the right amount of fresh air depending on its usage. The aim of regulating the quantity of air has resulted in the use of various mechanical systems. We distinguish between full air-conditioning, partial air-conditioning and ventilation systems (which feed untreated outside air into the interior) depending on the scope of the air-treatment measures. In air-conditioning systems the air is heated, cooled, humidified and dehumidified; such systems enable any desired internal climate to be realised regardless of the external conditions. The air-treatment measures in partial air-conditioning systems are reduced – the installation regulates between one and three parameters.

The use of a ventilation system is frequently only discussed in connection with the potential energy-savings achieved by reducing the ventilation heat losses. However, the problem more often is not one of too much ventilation, but rather too little, i.e. the provision of oxygen and the removal of pollutants and moisture is no longer secured. Guaranteeing an adequate air change rate to avoid unhygienic conditions is becoming more and more crucial as building envelopes become ever more tightly sealed. It has often been observed that the ventilation habits of users remain unchanged after the installation of new, sealed windows. However, the air change rate of the new windows is much lower than that of the old, leaky ones. The ensuing tendency for a higher humidity in the interior can then lead to a relative humidity that might offer good conditions for mould growth on cooler surfaces (thermal bridges). It is also frequently forgotten that in non-residential

buildings in particular, controlling the quantity of incoming air in the summer reduces the temperature rise in the interior. But windows opened in the mornings in summer are often not closed again even after the outside temperature has climbed well above the room temperature.

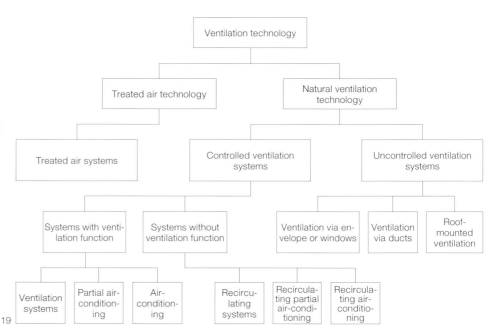

19

19   The diagram above (from DIN 1946) illustrates the possible forms of ventilation. There are important differences between natural ventilation (uncontrolled ventilation systems) and mechanical ventilation (controlled ventilation systems). In the latter, we distinguish between systems that work with and without the introduction of outside air (systems with and without ventilation function).

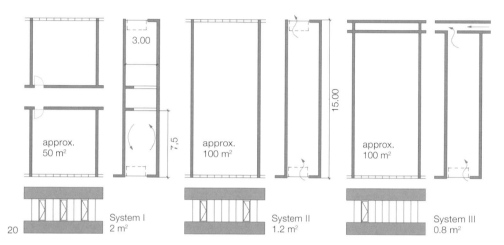

Natural ventilation
A natural flow through the building can only be achieved in an architectural concept that has been optimised in terms of dynamic fluid flows. Room depths and heights, the sizes of window openings and the local wind conditions are the parameters that can influence the functional, constructional and also architectural concept of a building.

The flow processes of natural ventilation can be simulated under various boundary conditions and then optimised. But even without elaborate simulation, the German Places of Work Guidelines can be used to determine the basic conditions a building has to fulfil (depending on its use) so that it can be ventilated naturally.
If night-time ventilation is being used in the summer, the ability of the ventilation openings to withstand adverse weather conditions, and also intruders, is a key issue because otherwise ventilation via the windows is simply not possible.

Even if the building concept is optimised with respect to good ventilation options, natural ventilation only works if the users are disciplined in their habits. Programmable top-light openers are being used increasingly in residential buildings to ensure regular ventilation regardless of the users' habits.

Ventilation cross-sections for ventilation according to German Places of Work Guidelines

System	Clear headroom H	Max. permissible room depth[1] related to clear headroom H [m]	Cross-section related to floor area[2] [m²], fresh-air and exhaust-air sizes identical [cm²/m²]		
			Room group A	Room group B	Room group C
I	≤ 4 m	2,5 × H	200	350	500
II		5,0 × H[3]	120	200	300
III			80	140	200
IV	> 4 m		80	140	200

[1] This column specifies the maximum depth of room for which various systems of uncontrolled ventilation can still be used depending on the height of the room.
[2] The figures given are in each case valid for the cross-sectional sizes of inlet and exhaust openings.
[3] In systems II, III and IV, the maximum permissible depth of room applies to the distance between the external walls and/or the ventilation openings in the duct or on the roof.

It should be possible to adjust (reduce) the ventilation cross-sections.

System I: Single-sided ventilation
System II: Cross-ventilation (openings on both sides or one side plus roof opening)
System III: Cross-ventilation (opening on one side and duct opposite)
System IV: Cross-ventilation (openings on both sides or one side plus roof opening)
Room group A: Sedentary activities (offices etc.)
Room group B: Non-sedentary activities (sales etc.)
Room group C: Activities with severe odour loads and heavy work

20 Building concepts that can be ventilated naturally according to the German Places of Work Guidelines

Controlled ventilation

In the simplest form of controlled ventilation, frequently employed in residential buildings, the fresh air enters the room via controllable openings in the window surround or in the external wall (extract system). On the exhaust-air side, a central fan is provided which continuously extracts the air from the interior. The exhaust-air duct should be located as close as possible to the centre of the apartment, preferably in the sanitary area. This means that internal wet rooms without windows no longer require the high-performance extractor fan so often encountered these days. Air flows under the doors create a current to carry away the exhaust air within each apartment, i.e. without the need for ventilation ducts. Heat recovery is possible in this arrangement by using an air-to-water heat pump which can extract the heat from the exhaust air.

A true extract system can also be retrofitted easily in existing buildings by using existing air ducts. The provision of continuous extraction at the end of the duct means that the ventilation can operate irrespective of the weather conditions.

Controlled ventilation with heat recovery

A direct exchange of heat between hot exhaust air and cold external air is only possible when a system of pipes is used to distribute the fresh air throughout the interior. It is advisable in such concepts to provide one ventilation unit for each apartment because the heat recovery gains can only be used by the respective heat consumer. These systems can also be operated with a ground coupling for preheating the air in winter or precooling the air in summer.

Controlled ventilation with heat recovery can be retrofitted in refurbishment projects. Generally, the installation of fresh-air ducts involves a loss of approx. 150 mm headroom in the rooms. In existing buildings the answer is to provide ducts in the corridors which then supply fresh air to the rooms via openings above the doors (include noise attenuators!).

Extraction is carried out in the sanitary areas without the need for an independent network of pipes.

One special form of ventilation with heat recovery is the individual unit that can be mounted on an external wall to serve just one room. Such units are primarily used when individual rooms are exposed to severe external noise and ventilation via the windows is not always possible.

21 Ventilation systems are not only sensible from the energy efficiency viewpoint – they can also have a positive effect on sound insulation and the relative humidity of the air.

Forms of ventilation			
	Natural	**Controlled[1]** (central exhaust-air installation)	**Controlled, with heat recovery[1]** (local installations for each apartment)
Air supply	too much too little	adjustable	adjustable
Heat recovery	not possible	possible (central exhaust-air heat pump)	readily possible (exhaust air to outside air)
Moisture regulation	limited	readily possible	readily possible
Filtering of the air	not possible	limited	optimum options
Sound insulation (external noise)	not possible	limited	optimum options
Sound insulation (system noise)	readily possible	limited (Leakage openings)	possible (install sound attenuators)
Affect on building		little work	much work (fresh-air distribution)
Passive preheating	not possible	limited (extraction via buffer)	optimum options (ground coupling, air coll.)
Operation	heavily dependent on users	not dependent on users (basic ventilation)	can be regulated independently of users
Night-time ventilation	limited (weather/intruder protection)	no problem	no problem
Costs		10–20 €/m²	50–80 €/m²

21 [1] Ventilation to DIN 18017 is not required for internal bathrooms.

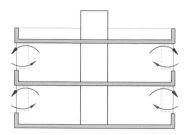

22 a

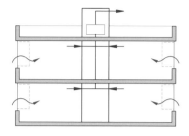

b

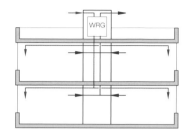

c

Energy efficiency evaluation

Assessing a ventilation system in terms of its energy efficiency takes place on two different levels:

On the one hand, a ventilation system – through its controlled supply of external air – reduces the energy demands that would otherwise have to be covered by heating or cooling systems. But on the other hand, the savings are lessened to a certain extent because the fans require electricity to run them.

These two influences are recorded and compared in the evaluation. In doing so, it is important to compare not only the final energy of the electricity requirement for the fans with the energy-savings for heating or cooling, but rather to consider and

compare the two values in terms of their use of raw materials by way of the primary energy factor. The final energy consumption of the fans must therefore be multiplied by a primary energy factor of 3, whereas the energy savings are assessed using the primary energy factor of the material with which they were generated.

22 Ventilation concepts
  a Natural ventilation
  b Controlled ventilation
  c Controlled ventilation with heat recovery
23 The table shows examples of annual energy balances for natural ventilation, controlled ventilation and controlled ventilation with heat recovery. The respective savings can be determined via the factors price of energy, capital cost of installation and increase in price of energy.
The examples are based on the following assumptions:
350 m² floor space, 2.50 m clear headroom, 185 heating days, 90% degree of efficiency, heating price 0.70 €/m³, electricity price 0.17 €/kWh, energy price inflation 5%, installation lifetime 20 years, interest rate 4%; fan output 0.2 W/m³ for exhaust-air operation and 0.5 W/m³ for fresh- and exhaust-air operation.

Energy efficiency evaluation – Ventilation

	Natural	Controlled[1]	Controlled, with heat recovery[2]
Heating			
heating requirement [kWh]	28000	24000	18000
heating energy requirement [kWh]	31111	26666	20000
energy source	Gas	Gas	Gas
cost of heating energy [€]	2178	1866	1400
primary energy [kWh]	34222	29333	22000
Auxiliary energy			
electricity requirement [kWh]	–	311	777
energy source		Electricity	Electricity
cost of auxiliary energy [€]		53	132
primary energy [kWh]		933	2331
Balance			
total primary energy [kWh]	34222	30266	24331
total costs [€]	2178	1919	1532
Savings			
(with respect to natural ventilation)			
costs [€]		259	646
primary energy [kWh]		3956	9891
Costs/benefits			
costs over 20 years (annuity)[3] [€]		8832	26500
cost-savings over 20 years [€]		8992	22428

[1] Infiltration air change rate 0.15, installation air change rate 0.4
[2] Infiltration air change rate 0.2, installation air change rate 0.4
[3] Exhaust-air installation € 6,000, fresh-/exhaust-air installation € 18,000; the cost of ventilation for internal bathrooms (DIN 18017) must be subtracted from this because it is compulsory anyway.

23

Lighting

Use of daylight

When calculating the energy performance of buildings, the energy requirement for artificial lighting plays a major role in non-residential buildings. As in every type of installation, the amount of energy required for operating a lighting system initially depends on the constructional concept.

The depth and height of a room, the arrangement, distribution and size of windows, the nature of any sunshades and, last but not least, the colour and properties of the internal surfaces determine the quantity and quality of daylight within the interior. The use of systems to (re)direct daylight can distribute the light more evenly throughout the depth of the room. The orientation of window areas depends on the purpose for which the windows have been included. The quality of a specific view of the outside world cannot be measured and therefore cannot be compared with the measurable magnitude of the energy requirement that is linked to the size and orientation of the window areas.

Whereas in residential buildings, south-facing windows are clearly preferred from the energy point of view, such a generalisation does not necessarily apply to a non-residential building.

In residential buildings, reducing heat losses in winter through windows in the north elevation is a crucial factor for the energy balance, which is why the size and orientation of openings must be optimised. By contrast, in an office building, generously sized windows on the north side are advisable in order to exploit all available light during long periods of occupation. Lowering the heat gains in summer and the even distribution of daylight play a much greater role here – in energy terms – than trying to reduce the heat losses.

Optimising the window area therefore depends on the compass direction and the use of the rooms. However, the respective mutual dependencies of the individual parameters cannot be generalised; instead, they must be checked for each individual case in the context of the specific boundary conditions.

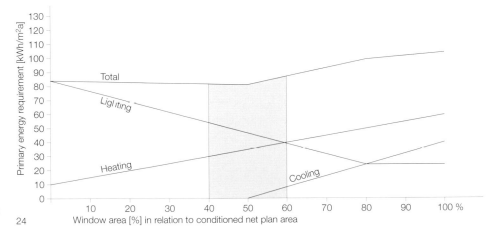

24 Primary energy requirement for a standard office room as a function of the window area (standard of insulation to Energy Conservation Act, south-facing windows with external sunblinds, heating by means of gas-fired condensing boiler, cooling by means of compression-type chiller)

25 The efficiency of a lighting system depends on, among other things, the lighting concept. Indirect lighting is always accompanied by a higher power consumption for the same level of illumination. The requirements for lighting systems are specified in DIN EN 12665 "Light and lighting – Basic terms and criteria for specifying lighting requirements" and DIN EN 12464 "Light and lighting – Lighting of work places" (e.g. 500 lx nominal lighting intensity at an office workplace).
   a Direct lighting
   b Indirect lighting
   c Direct lighting with additional task lighting
   d Task lighting with indirect general lighting
26 Performance and annual consumption of different lighting systems

Artificial lighting

When planning artificial lighting, it is the ergonomics, aesthetics and energy consumption aspects which are important. In this book we shall consider exclusively the energy-related effects. The energy requirement for artificial lighting is determined by the so-called operating time of the lighting units, the direct and indirect lighting proportions, the technology of the lamps, the type of lamps and their controls.

The operating time can be reduced through optimum use of daylight in conjunction with demand- and occupancy-based controls. It is frequently the case that the artificial lighting is designed so that the area to be illuminated is not lit directly but rather indirectly by reflecting the light off surfaces in the room because this generates an even, essentially non-glare illumination, and creates a pleasant lighting atmosphere. However, it is frequently forgotten that high indirect proportions lead to increased lighting requirements and hence to an increase of about 20% in the electricity consumption. The most common types of lamps for building interiors, listed according to their efficiency, are: fluorescent lamps, LEDs, halogen lamps and incandescent lamps. Fluorescent lamps are operated with a ballast resistor, but an electronic ballast resistor achieves a further energy saving of approx. 20% compared to a conventional ballast resistor. And daylight-dependent dimming, which is possible with electronic ballast resistors, can bring an additional energy saving of up to 50%.

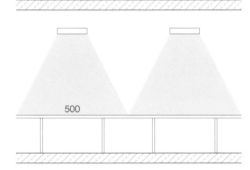

25 a

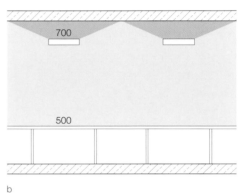

b

c

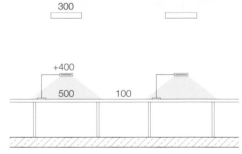

d

Energy efficiency evaluation – lighting
(window area 50%, light-coloured surfaces, room depth 5 m, office use, 100 m² net floor area)

		Connected load [W/m²]	Full operating hours [h]	Final energy [kWh]	Ressource	Primary energy [kWh]	CO_2-emiss. [kg]
1	Old system	25	2000	5000	Electricity	15000	3235
2	New system, EBR	14	2000	2800	Electricity	8400	1811
3	New system, EBR daylight control and presence detector	14	1600	2240	Electricity	6720	1450
4	New system as for No. 3, but indirect	18	1600	2880	Electricity	8640	1863
5	New system as for No. 3, but direct and with workplace-based switching zones	10	1600	1600	Electricity	4800	1035
6	New system as for No. 5, with daylight (re)direction	10	1200	1000	Electricity	3000	647

26   EBR = electronic ballast resistor

Examples

The refurbishment, conversion or upgrading of existing buildings always involves energy-efficiency issues. However, these cannot be considered in isolation from the other aspects of planning and design, nor solved by specialists with a narrow remit. This is because the energy-related matters are closely linked with the functional, constructional, economic and – of course – also the architectural demands placed on a sustainable concept. An optimisation that unites quality, user acceptance and durability can therefore only be successful when considered in this holistic context.

It is precisely the complex and often conflicting requirements placed on buildings as well as the rising cost of energy that make it imperative to seek synergies in refurbishment work in order to achieve added value in both economic and ecological terms.

The case studies on the following pages illustrate the level of quality that can be achieved when a refurbishment project is initially analysed from the conceptual viewpoint, i.e. holistically, and then further developed taking into account energy, mechanical services and lighting issues. The concepts shown here range from a simple energy-efficiency improvement for a building envelope to extensions or even demolition work. Specific issues, like in the upgrading of the terrace house near Zürich, show how individual overall concepts devised for a specific building can lead to a high-quality result.

It will become clear to the reader that sustainable planning and building is impossible without the help of an architect with a full portfolio of skills.

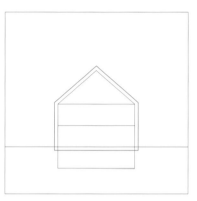
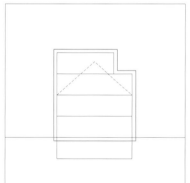
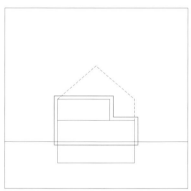

Examples

Wasgenring School, Basel

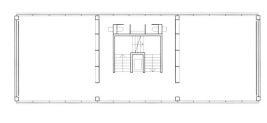

Architects: Fritz and Bruno Haller (existing building)
Facade: PPEngineering Petignat (Facade technology, Riehen, Switzerland (overall planning of refurbishment)
Completion: 1960, 2004–2005

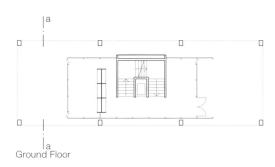

aa

a
a
Ground Floor

1st–4th floors

Architecture

The idea of the flowing space, which permits ambiguous interpretations, forms the core of this urban configuration. The relationship between the individual blocks is based on a precise geometrical arrangement. The two four-storey classroom blocks together with the adjoining low-rise structures stake out the spatial centre of the complex.

The two building types develop independently within the framework of the underlying geometrical system. The north and south facades of the classroom

blocks are fully glazed. Placing the sanitary facilities in the basement and the stairs and lift in the centre of each block made the homogenous facade design possible; its architectural expression by combining only two different elements.

The structural and architectural concepts of the individual blocks are governed by the same principle – the separation and subsequent structured joining of individual functional elements.

As a consequence of the rigorous original conception – from the urban design to the building technology – the facade renovation was subject to stringent guidelines.

Passive concept

Existing construction

A reinforced concrete frame forms the loadbearing structure. The east and west elevations utilise masonry infill panels, whereas the north and south sides are fully glazed – storey-high fixed glazing elements in steel frames, some of which are divided into four equal lights which include a pair of hopper-type opening lights. The original single glazing was replaced in the 1980s with double glazing. Louvre blinds were added to the south side to control the amount of incoming heat and light.

This concept resulted in a high heating energy consumption in winter and severe solar heat gains in the summer. However, the basic idea of glazing to the north and south elevations is a good one; an east-west orientation would have led to a more rapid faster temperature rise in the classrooms in summer because the external heat loads would have started in the early morning and continued until late evening. In 2003 the school authorities decided to refurbish the buildings with the stipulation that the mullion dimensions not be altered.

Refurbishment

The task of the refurbishment project was to improve the level of thermal comfort in the classrooms without reducing the amount of glazing or installing additional mechanical plant.

A competition was held to find the best solution, a facade with elements made from aluminium sections with a thermal break was chosen. Despite the new frame construction, the width of the frame components remained unchanged so that the overall architectural impression of the facade was retained. Solar-control glass with a g-value of 42%, a τ-value of 68% and a U-value of 1.1 W/m^2K (U_g) was

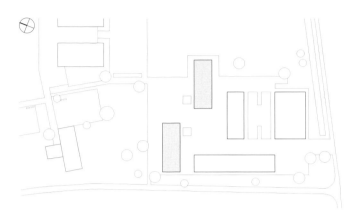

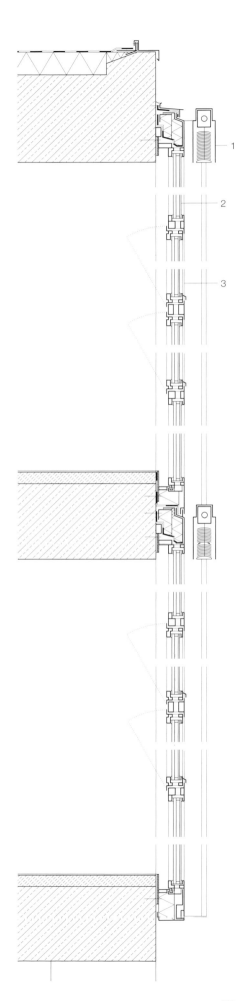

Section, plans
scale 1:400
Location plan
scale 1:2000

Vertical section through south facade
scale 1:20

1 sunblind
   80 mm louvres
2 fixed light
   solar-control glass
   8 mm float glass + 16 mm cavity + laminated
   safety glass (= 2 x 6 mm toughened safety
   glass)
3 hopper-type opening light
   solar-control glass
   8 mm float glass + 16 mm cavity + laminated
   safety glass (= 2 x 6 mm toughened safety
   glass)

selected for the new glazing.
Thermal insulation to the plain east and
west ends of each block was not implemented. The roof had already been
upgraded with an extra 120 mm of thermal insulation at an earlier date. It was
also not possible to remove the sound
insulation elements fitted to the soffits of
the suspended floor slabs, which means
that the storage mass available can be
activated to a limited extent only. Therefore, the deficiencies in the thermal comfort so often associated with fully glazed
facades could not be fully overcome.

Active concept

Existing construction
The building is heated by a hot-water
heating system which uses the waste
heat of a nearby waste incinerator.
Thanks to the interior layout (depth of
rooms, cross-ventilation), natural ventilation has always been possible in the
classroom blocks. In summer the fresh air
was drawn from the north side, in winter
from the south side. Manual, occasional
ventilation by opening windows in both
facades was possible and efficient.

Refurbishment
No additional mechanical plant was
installed, merely the addition of modern
control technology to optimise the natural
ventilation. All the opening lights have
been fitted with programmable electric
openers. The motors are operated
depending on internal temperature, CO_2
content of interior air, wind speed, external temperature and rain so that an adequate air change rate is achieved while
avoiding energy losses or excessive heat
gains through unnecessary ventilation.
The weather-based control also permits
night-time ventilation. To optimise the
supply of fresh air, the system is set to
open at 6 a.m. every morning and during
each of the breaks between lessons.

Verification

To facilitate comparisons between the refurbishment projects shown here, the energy performance calculations are carried out according to the regulations valid in Germany. The differentiated calculation of the theoretical U-values for glazing to DIN ISO 10077-1 is of interest in this context.

The calculation considers an element measuring 1.70 x 2.92 m. The U-value of the frame U_f calculated by the manufacturer according to DIN ISO 10077-2 is 1.50 W/m²K for the fixed elements and 1.65 W/m²K for the elements with two opening lights. Based on these two values, the U-value of the glass itself (U_g = 1.1 W/m²K) and the value for the hermetic edge seal, we obtain U-values for the whole window Uw,BW of 1.3 W/m²K for the fixed and 1.4 W/m²K for the elements with opening lights. These values are well below the maximum value of 1.7 W/m²K specified in the component analysis method for upgrading projects. Verification of the summertime thermal performance in combination with the external sunblinds also results in favourable figures.

Building data

	Existing building	Refurbished building
Basic data		
Energy reference area	900 m²	900 m²
Heated volume	3340 m³	3340 m³
Enclosing surface area	1490 m²	1490 m²
No. of pupils	200	200
Volume of air	2500 m³	2500 m³
Air change rate	2	1
Passive concept		
Soil to unheated space	1.4 W/m²K	1.4 W/m²K
Wall	1.33 W/m²K	1.33 W/m²K
Roof	0.3 W/m²K	0.3 W/m²K
Windows	2.8 W/m²K	1.3/1.4 W/m²K
g-value	0.8	0.5
F_c-value	0.25	0.18
Active concept		
Final energy		
Heating	180 kWh/m²a	140 kWh/m²a
Resource	district heating	district heating
Hot water (not included in energy onservation assessment)	–	–
Cooling	–	–
Lighting	8 kWh/m²a	8 kWh/m²a
Ventilation	natural	natural (controlled)
Auxiliary energy		
Pumps	4 kWh/m²a	3 kWh/m²a
Ecology (according to GEMIS and DIN 4701-10)		
CO_2	47 kg CO_2/m²a	37 kg CO_2/m²a
Primary energy	162 kWh/m²a	131 kWh/m²a
Economy		
Energy cost-savings		2,000 €/year

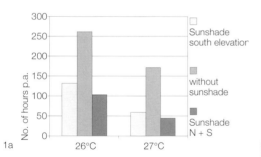

1a

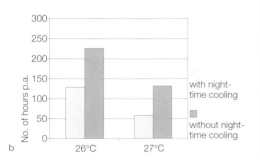

b

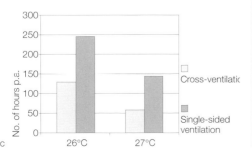

c

1   In this project, computer simulations were employed to investigate various building standards (sunshading, lighting) and different natural ventilation principles with respect to their effects on the temperature rise internally. The results show that the heat loads in summer can be substantially reduced by optimising the passive concept.

a   No. of hours p.a. during which the building is used with internal temperatures > 26°C and > 27°C, in each case with and without sunshading.

b   No. of hours p.a. during which the building is used with internal temperatures > 26°C and > 27°C, with and without night-time cooling by way of natural ventilation.

c   No. of hours p.a. during which the building is used with internal temperatures > 26°C and > 27°C, with cross-ventilation and single-sided ventilation.

Terrace house near Zürich

Architects: Harder & Spreyermann, Zürich
Engineers: Basler & Hofmann, Zürich
Building performance: Zehnder & Kälin, Zürich
Completion: 1966, 2005

Architecture

This terrace house is situated on an estate erected in 1966; the prevailing impression is one of fair-face concrete and facing brickwork. As part of an extensive refurbishment project, the house shown here was treated to an energy-efficiency upgrade and given a new interior layout. Non-loadbearing internal walls were removed or repositioned, the facade to the courtyard was glazed and the whole rather compartmentalised interior turned into a more spacious continuum. The only way to improve the energy balance was through internal measures because the external appearance and the constructional transitions to the neighbouring houses had to remain untouched.

Passive concept

Existing construction

The building had not been altered since it was first built and the standards no longer complied with today's requirements. Furthermore, in order to maintain the value of the building, a fundamental overhaul of all non-loadbearing components was essential, which meant that an energy-efficiency upgrade could be carried out as part of an overall programme of measures for a permanent improvement.

Refurbishment

The "Minergie" quality standard – introduced by the Swiss cantons of Zürich and Bern – denotes goods and services that enable a rational use of energy and the extensive use of renewable energy while at the same time reducing the environmental impact and raising living standards.

Specifically, the final energy consumption should be reduced by 25% and the consumption of fossil fuels cut by 50% with respect to the average state of the art. In order to achieve the "Minergie" standard

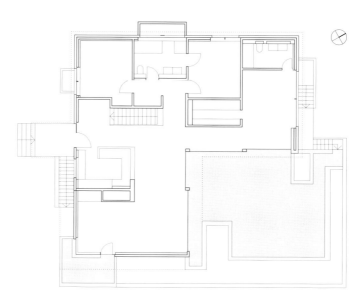

Ground (upper) floor

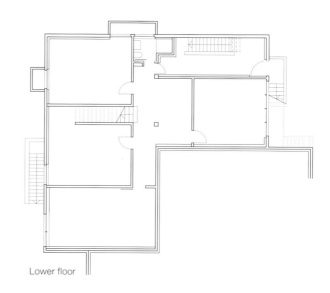

Plans
scale 1:250   Lower floor

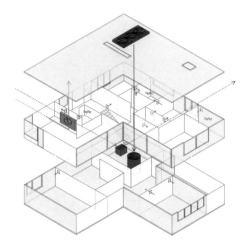

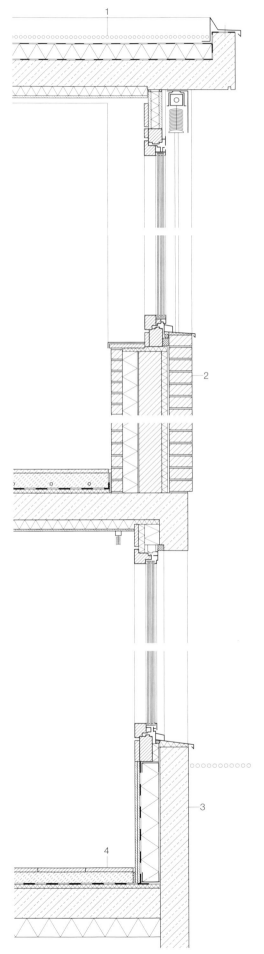

☐ Optimised thermal insulation

■ Open fireplace

■ Hot-water provision
(solar collector + tank)
≈ Hot-water take-off point

■ Ventilation for controlling thermal comfort
➤ Fresh air
➤ Exhaust air
➤ Leakage air

Source: MINERGIE

in the existing building stock, the primary energy requirement for heating, hot water and ventilation should not exceed 80 kWh/m²a after refurbishment.

As the external appearance could not be altered, the house was insulated from the inside. On the upper (i.e. ground) floor, 120 mm of thermal insulation (mineral-fibre boards) was installed behind a leaf of facing brickwork. On the lower floor, the insulation was improved by installing composite panels comprising 120 mm thick polystyrene and a wooden facing. The roof insulation was upgraded by adding 80 mm outside and 60 mm to the soffit inside. All the windows were replaced with triple-glazed units.

Active concept

Existing construction

Up until the time of refurbishment, the heating and hot-water requirements had been provided exclusively via a district heating system.

Refurbishment

Besides the alterations to the construction, it was also necessary to upgrade the installations in order to meet the "Minergie" standard. The installation is considered in the "Minergie" limiting value, which

roughly corresponds to the primary energy parameter used in Germany. The given limiting value of 80 kWh/m²a can be achieved with the district heating setup plus solar collectors for the hot water. Controlled ventilation of the interior with heat recovery was also part of the HVAC concept. The new heating system is operated with a flow/return temperature of 40/32°C. On the ground floor, the heat is distributed via a new underfloor heating system. During very cold weather, this system is backed up by an open fireplace whose solid construction can store a portion of the heat and emit it later. The existing radiators were retained on the lower floor.

In energy-efficiency terms, it is sensible to separate the hot-water provision from the district heating system during the warmer months when the house is not being heated. Operating the district heating installation just for hot water requirements is extremely inefficient owing to the high distribution losses and the auxiliary energy required for the pumps. During these periods, the solar collectors and an electric booster heater are used to generate the heat required.

Verification

Verification according to the German Energy Conservation Act is no problem in this case owing to the high energy-efficiency quality of the refurbished house. The primary energy parameter called for in the Swiss "Minergie" standard is so high that it is comparable with the standard for new building work laid down by the Energy Conservation Act. As the thermal insulation measures also achieve the limiting value HT' valid for new buildings, the house can be designated a "low-energy house within the existing building stock".

Section through facade
scale 1:20

1 roof construction:
40 mm gravel
2 layers of bitumen sheeting
80 mm thermal insulation
vapour barrier
160 mm reinforced concrete slab (existing)
50 mm insulation
12.5 mm plasterboard
2 wall construction, ground floor:
120 mm clay facing brickwork
10 mm cavity
30 mm thermal insulation (existing)
5 mm mortar-based adhesive
115 mm calcium silicate brickwork (existing)
80 mm thermal insulation
62.5 mm inner leaf
3 wall construction, lower floor:
150 mm reinforced concrete (existing)
5 mm mortar-based adhesive
100 mm thermal insulation
2 No. 12.5 mm plasterboard
4 floor construction, lower floor:
22 mm wood-block flooring, oiled cherrywood
60 mm screed
separating layer
20 mm impact sound insulation
160 mm reinforced concrete (existing)
100 mm thermal insulation (existing)

Building data

	Existing building	Refurbished building
Basic data		
Energy reference area	250 m²	250 m²
Heated volume	675 m³	675 m³
Enclosing surface area	580 m²	580 m²
Volume of air	600 m³	600 m³
Air change rate	1	0.5
Passive concept		
Soil to unheated space	1.0 W/m²K	0.40 W/m²K
Wall	1.2 W/m²K	0.40 W/m²K
Roof	1.2 W/m²K	0.34 W/m²K
Windows	3.0 W/m²K	0.80 W/m²K
Doors	3.0	2.00
g-value	0.80	0.50
F_c-value		0.12
Active concept		
Final energy		
Heating	160 kWh/m²a	82 kWh/m²a
Resource	district heating	district heating
Hot water	40 kWh/m²a	5 kWh/m²a
Resource	district heating	district heating, electricity, solar
Auxiliary energy		
Pumps	3 kWh/m²a	2 kWh/m²a
Fans (ventilation)	–	4 kWh/m²a
Ecology		
(to GEMIS and DIN 4701-10)		
CO_2	45 kg CO_2/m²a	23 kg CO_2/m²a
Primary energy	150 kWh/m²a	80 kWh/m²a
Economy		
Energy cost-savings		500 €/year

Office building, Zürich

Architects: Romero & Schäfle, Zürich
Engineers: Amstein + Walthert AG, Zürich
Building physics: Amstein + Walthert AG, Zürich
Completion: 1970, 2001

Architecture

The refurbishment of this office block built in 1970 is a good example of how an energy-efficiency upgrade is especially effective when it forms part of a programme of permanent improvement measures. In this project the measures included an increase in the usable floor area and substantial improvements to the quality of the working environment, as well as improving the building performance and raising the standard of the conditioning and lighting installations. A flexible interior layout has been realised which fulfils the prerequisites for prolonged utilisation of the building because it can be easily adapted to suit changing requirements. The continuous windows placed in front of the columns of the loadbearing frame updated the building's image. An apparently low-value property has been turned into a high-quality business location through this comprehensive refurbishment.

Passive concept

Existing construction

Owing to the condition of the construction, the outdated interior and inefficient installations, the offices could only be let at low rents.

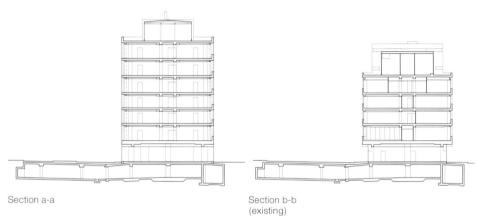

Section a-a

Section b-b
(existing)

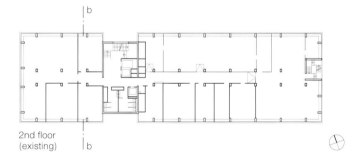

2nd floor
(existing)

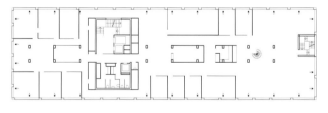

2nd floor

Plans,
sections
scale 1:750

Ground floor

Vertical section
scale 1:20

1 roof construction:
   gravel
   2 x bitumen sheeting
   160 mm cellular glass thermal insulation
   vapour barrier
   260 mm reinforced concrete
2 straight-arm textile awning
3 triple glazing:
   12 mm toughened safety glass + 12 mm cavity +
   8 mm toughened safety glass + 12 mm cavity +
   9 mm laminated safety glass
   g-value 0.40
   τ-value 0.72
   U_g 0.80 W/m²K, $U_{w,BW}$ = 1.2 W/m²K
4 wall construction:
   4 mm sheet aluminium on
   40 mm deep sheet steel backing
   120 mm thermal insulation
   150 mm reinforced concrete (existing)
   3 mm sheet aluminium on
   20 mm deep sheet steel backing

5 triple glazing:
   15 mm toughened safety glass + 100 mm cavity +
   8 mm toughened safety glass + 13 mm cavity +
   8 mm toughened safety glass
   g-value 0.40
   τ-value 0.72
   U_g 0.80 W/m²K, $U_{w,BW}$ = 1.2 W/m²K
6 floor construction:
   15 mm wood-block flooring
   180 mm access floor
   300 mm reinforced concrete (existing)

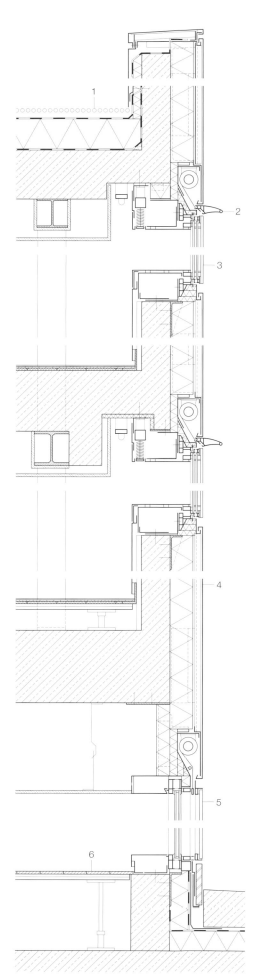

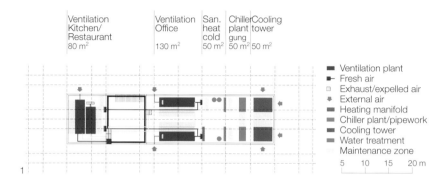

Ventilation Kitchen/ Restaurant 80 m²	Ventilation Office 130 m²	San. heat cold 50 m²	Chiller plant gung 50 m²	Cooling tower 50 m²

- Ventilation plant
- Fresh air
- Exhaust/expelled air
- External air
- Heating manifold
- Chiller plant/pipework
- Cooling tower
- Water treatment
- Maintenance zone

5   10   15   20 m

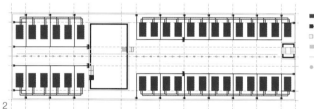

- Cooling and heating ceiling
- Fresh air
- Exhaust/expelled air
- Electrics distribution for storey
- Cable duct
- Downlights

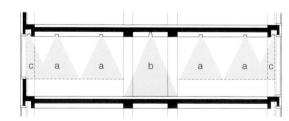

a Working zone with recesses lighting (timer + presence detection)
b Access zone with recessed lighting (timer)
c Facade zone with strip of fluorescent tubes for spotlighting (daylight control)

d South, east and west facades with external shading in the form of fabric awnings
e Internal anti-glare screen on all facades
f High and even daylight quotient in working zone
g No shading on north facade

1 Roof-mounted central plant room
2 Installation layout in suspended ceiling
   Horizontal distribution of fresh air is carried out only beneath the soffit of the topmost storey (6th floor). From here the vertical distribution is behind the metal mullions of the window strips.
3 Artificial lighting concept
4 Daylighting concept

Refurbishment

Firstly, the usable floor space of the building was increased by adding two storeys, closing the gap in the longitudinal facade and eliminating the shopping arcades at ground floor level.

The level of daylight in the interior was increased considerably by reducing the concrete spandrel panels on the south, east and west sides and removing them completely on the north elevation. The "dummy columns" on the facade were also removed. High-quality external insulation, with weather protection in the form of sheet aluminium separated by an air cavity, has replaced the internal insulation. The new windows with their fixed lights are fitted with glazing with optimum thermal and light transmittance values. The sunblinds in the form of straight-arm awnings offer ideal shading but at the same time still ensure a high level of daylight and a good view of the surroundings. When retracted, the awnings are hardly noticeable externally because they are completely covered and hence protected from the weather.

The horizontal window strips are divided up by vertical mullions which conceal, behind sheet metal, opening vents for local ventilation. As the sheet metal panels provide protection from the weather and intruders, the vents can also remain open when the building is not occupied (nights, weekends) to assist natural ventilation and heat dissipation.

Active concept

Existing construction

Apart from a few small improvements, the installations still reflected the standards of 1970. The building was heated by an oil-fired boiler located in the basement, whereas the air-conditioning plant and chillers were mounted on the roof. Cooling was exclusively by means of air, heating via convector under the windows.

Heat recovery was non-existent. The interior conditioning concept resulted in a very high air change rate, especially in summer, with a correspondingly high electricity consumption. The lighting was outdated and likewise led to a high electricity consumption.

Refurbishment
All the installations have been renewed and are now situated in a compact new rooftop plant room. Heating and cooling is now by way of combined heating/cooling ceilings which use only water – an efficient heat transfer fluid. The ventilation plant with heat recovery is now used exclusively for supplying fresh air to the interior and so can be operated with a single air change rate. Pretreatment of the incoming air also makes a minor contribution to heating and cooling. The lighting has been redesigned. In order to achieve the desired flexibility in the layout of office equipment and furniture, the lighting installation in the office zones has been designed so that a level of illumination of 500 lx is available at every point.

Verification
The concept for this building was verified according to the regulations valid in Switzerland. If we transfer the results to pre-standard DIN V 18599, which in future will be applicable for non-residential buildings in Germany, then the primary energy parameter (see table above) is the benchmark for the energy performance of the building. At 142 kWh/m²a, this building represents a high energy standard for a non-residential property.

Building data

	Existing building	Refurbished building
Basic data		
Energy reference area	4500 m²	6200 m²
Heated volume	19500 m³	27500 m³
Enclosing surface area	4800 m²	6200 m²
Workstations	300	400
Volume of air	14000 m³	19000 m³
Air change rate	1	1
Passive concept		
Soil to unheated space	1.6 W/m²K	0.4 W/m²K
Wall	1.2 W/m²K	0.4 W/m²K
Roof	1.0 W/m²K	0.3 W/m²K
Wiindows	2.8 W/m²K	1.2 W/m²K
g-value	0.80	0.40
F_c-value	0.25	0.12
Active concept		
Final energy		
Heating	191 kWh/m²a	36 kWh/m²a
Source	oil	gas
Hot water	not assessed	not assessed
Source	district heating	solar/district heating
Cooling	24 kWh/m²a	10 kWh/m²a
Source	electricity	electricity
Lighting	50 kWh/m²a	18 kWh/m²a
Auxiliary energy		
Pumps	3 kWh/m²a	2 kWh/m²a
Fans (ventilation)	14 kWh/m²a	6 kWh/m²a
Ecology		
(to GEMIS and DIN 4701-10)		
CO_2	115 kg CO_2/m²a	32 kg CO_2/m²a
Primary energy	482 kWh/m²a	142 kWh/m²a
Economy		
Energy cost-savings		50,000 €/year

Electricity breakdown

	Existing building	Refurbished building
Total	**97 kWh/m²a**	**34 kWh/m²a**
Lighting	**50 kWh/m²a**	**18 kWh/m²a**
Power	25 W/m²	12 W/m²
Full operating hours p.a.	2500	1500
Cooling	**24 kWh/m²**	**10 kWh/m²**
Power	80 W/m²	50 W/m²
Full operating hours p.a.	600	400
Compression-type refrigeration unit		
(1 kWh electricity for 2 kWh cooling)		
Ventilation (fan)	**14 kWh/m²a**	**6 kWh/m²a**
vol/m²	3.5 m³	2.5 m³
Full operating hours p.a	800 h	800 h
Fan	5 W/m³	3 W/m³

Nursery school, Ulm

Architects: Günter Herrmann Architekten, Stuttgart
Engineers: Trippe & Partner,
Leinfelden-Echterdingen
Building physics: GFO Gesellschaft für bau-
physikalische Objektberatung, Krefeld
Completion: 1965, 2005

Upper floor

Ground floor

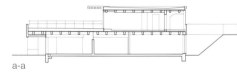

a-a

Plans, section
scale 1:500

Architecture

This parish centre dating from the 1960s consists of four separate buildings: nursery school, rectory, parish hall and church. All four buildings had to be totally refurbished in line with energy efficiency and sustainability criteria taking into account the overall architectural concept. Breaking down the refurbishment measures into individual phases rendered possible a step-by-step realisation. The overall impression of the complex in its urban setting has remained unchanged, but the facade refurbishment measures permit a new interpretation of the external form.

Passive concept

Existing construction
The nursery school will be used here as an example of the refurbishment concept. The building has a reinforced concrete frame and ribbed concrete floor slabs. The plain wall surfaces comprise precast concrete elements with integral insulation in a sandwich construction. Owing to the high heat losses, the thermal comfort problems and the high cost of upkeep, comprehensive refurbishment was essential.

Refurbishment
The heating requirement can be reduced considerably by insulating all enclosing surfaces and renewing the windows. Prior to installing the new insulation, the embedded energy of the materials used was investigated. This revealed that a facade with a ventilated cavity was particularly advantageous in terms of cost of upkeep and later demolition/changes. Separating the weather-protection layer from the insulating layer (no adhesive) fascilitates maintenance as compared to a thermal insulation composite system, and is easy to recycle in the event of demolition or modifications. As the Eternit facade panels chosen are highly resistant to

mechanical damage, the use of a lightweight mineral wool (thermal conductivity group 035) for the insulation does not pose a problem. And where necessary, it is easy to incorporate external louvre blinds behind the weatherproof outer leaf to ensure optimum sunshading without altering the external appearance.

Active concept

Existing construction
The parish hall is connected to a district heating system and so there was no need to make any alterations with regard to the heating plant.

Refurbishment
However, to improve the heat output (efficiency, thermal comfort), the radiators were renewed. In addition, a new ventilation system with heat recovery was installed in the nursery school. This new system cuts the heating requirement considerably and simultaneously ensures an optimum air quality in the activity rooms. These systems were supplemented by a decentralised solar energy system in the parish hall which covers about 65% of the heating requirement for hot-water provision.

Verification

An assessment according to the Energy Conservation Act is easy to carry out with the standard of insulation and the heating plant with its optimised primary energy parameter as implemented in this project. The specific transmission heat loss HT' related to the area of the enclosing surfaces is 35% lower than the maximum permissible value and at 60 kWh/m²a the primary energy requirement is likewise well below the maximum value. This building therefore satisfies even the KfW 60 standard (see p. 108).

Vertical section
scale 1:20

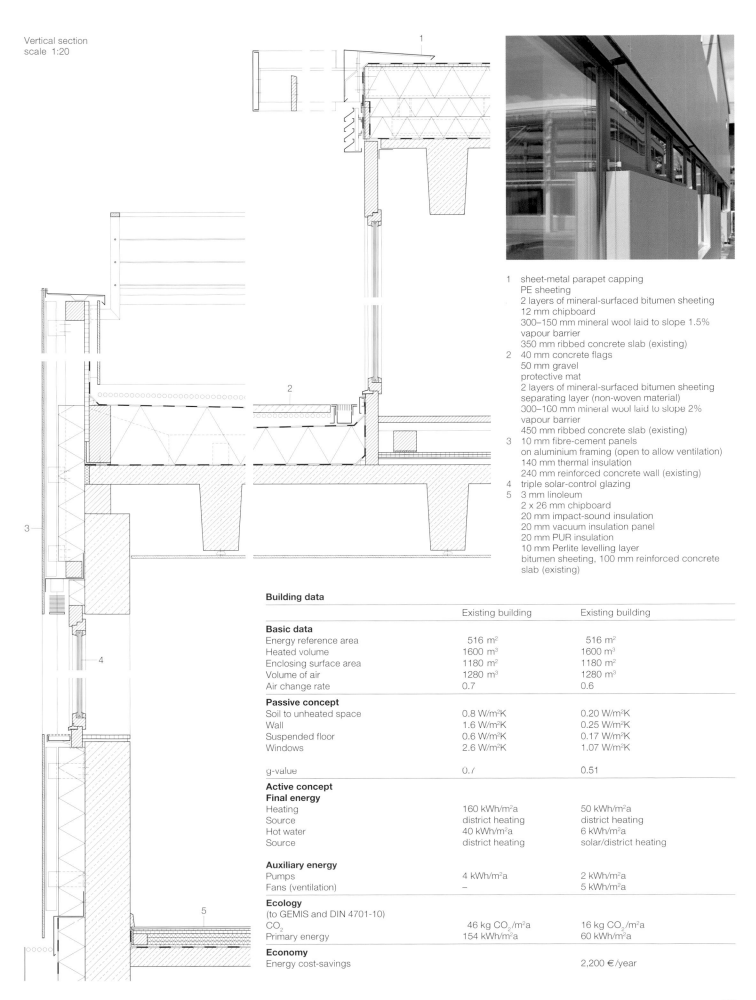

1 sheet-metal parapet capping
   PE sheeting
   2 layers of mineral-surfaced bitumen sheeting
   12 mm chipboard
   300–150 mm mineral wool laid to slope 1.5%
   vapour barrier
   350 mm ribbed concrete slab (existing)
2 40 mm concrete flags
   50 mm gravel
   protective mat
   2 layers of mineral-surfaced bitumen sheeting
   separating layer (non-woven material)
   300–160 mm mineral wool laid to slope 2%
   vapour barrier
   450 mm ribbed concrete slab (existing)
3 10 mm fibre-cement panels
   on aluminium framing (open to allow ventilation)
   140 mm thermal insulation
   240 mm reinforced concrete wall (existing)
4 triple solar-control glazing
5 3 mm linoleum
   2 x 26 mm chipboard
   20 mm impact-sound insulation
   20 mm vacuum insulation panel
   20 mm PUR insulation
   10 mm Perlite levelling layer
   bitumen sheeting, 100 mm reinforced concrete
   slab (existing)

Building data

	Existing building	Existing building
Basic data		
Energy reference area	516 m²	516 m²
Heated volume	1600 m³	1600 m³
Enclosing surface area	1180 m²	1180 m²
Volume of air	1280 m³	1280 m³
Air change rate	0.7	0.6
Passive concept		
Soil to unheated space	0.8 W/m²K	0.20 W/m²K
Wall	1.6 W/m²K	0.25 W/m²K
Suspended floor	0.6 W/m²K	0.17 W/m²K
Windows	2.6 W/m²K	1.07 W/m²K
g-value	0.7	0.51
Active concept		
Final energy		
Heating	160 kWh/m²a	50 kWh/m²a
Source	district heating	district heating
Hot water	40 kWh/m²a	6 kWh/m²a
Source	district heating	solar/district heating
Auxiliary energy		
Pumps	4 kWh/m²a	2 kWh/m²a
Fans (ventilation)	–	5 kWh/m²a
Ecology		
(to GEMIS and DIN 4701-10)		
CO₂	46 kg CO₂/m²a	16 kg CO₂/m²a
Primary energy	154 kWh/m²a	60 kWh/m²a
Economy		
Energy cost-savings		2,200 €/year

Rectory, Ampermoching

Architects: Clemens Richarz and Thomas Strunz,
               Munich
Engineer: Friedrich Hamp, Munich
Completion: 1724, 2001–2002

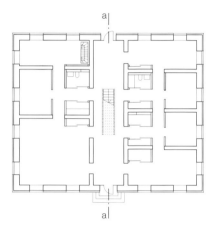

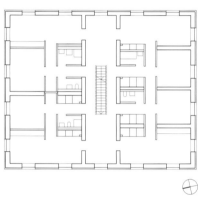

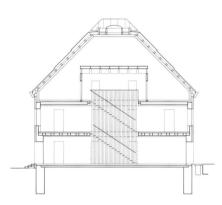

Architecture

The rectory designed in 1724 by the Baroque architect Johann Baptist Gunetzrhainer is today part of a village-style parish centre which features a new parish hall dating from the year 2000 alongside the old village church. As part of the new building work, the old rectory was refurbished and returned to its original Baroque form.

The crumbling roof structure was removed and replaced by the hipped roof originally envisaged by Gunetzrhainer (see elevation of 1724). In addition, the Baroque interior layout was re-created so that the associated facade geometry could also be restored. The entire plan layout is developed from a precise geometrical system. The compact arrangement of the sanitary facilities means that the classical theme of the enfilade can be taken up in the central hallway providing access to the various rooms. The parish office and various activity rooms are located on the ground floor, two apartments on the upper floor. The roof space is currently not habitable and is simply used for storage. However, the new roof structure does allow for conversion to a habitable space at a later date.

Passive concept

Existing construction

The walls of 400–600 mm clay brickwork were intact and adequate for supporting the load of the new roof structure, which spans the full width of the building. Just a few of the loadbearing timber joists to the upper floors had to be replaced and a concrete ring beam added to accommodate the horizontal thrust. The building had no insulation, some of the windows had single glazing, others were in the form of double-glazed windows. A precise architectural survey revealed that the external walls deviated by some 60–80 mm from the vertical and horizontal building lines.

Refurbishment

The inaccuracies in the external walls mentioned above were made good with a layer of 60–140 mm thermal insulation render, which had to be applied in several operations. However, with this process a uniform temperature on the inner surfaces of the external walls is not attained, a condition which could, at increased humiditiy lead to mould growth, especially at the geometrical thermal bridges. Controlled ventilation (see "Active concept" on p. 90) helps to remedy this

problem because the regular exchange of air keeps the relative humidity of the interior air so low that even components with a low surface temperature are not at risk. Thermal insulation was laid on the ground floor and insulation was placed between the joists of the suspended floor below the unheated roof space and incorporated in the floor finishes to the roof space. All the windows were renewed and fitted with folding wooden shutters internally, which provide a blackout option and also additional thermal insulation at night.

Plans, section,
elevation (1724)
scale 1:400
Section through facade
scale 1:20

1 roof construction:
   0.7 mm pre-weathered sheet titanium-zinc
   separating layer
   24 mm plain-edge boarding
   60/80 mm battens
   100/160 mm rafters
   IPE 220 steel section
2 10 mm acrylic sheet
3 ventilation outlet, 200 x 200 mm plywood
4 wall construction:
   60–140 mm thermal insulation render
   400–600 mm solid clay masonry
   30 mm lime-gypsum plaster
5 construction of floor to roof space:
   20 mm larch floorboards
   20 mm timber battens,
   with mineral wool insulation between
   22/20 mm mineral wool impact sound
   insulation
   22 mm chipboard
   40 mm battens
   2 x 10 mm fire protection boards
   22 mm plain-edge boarding
   240 mm timber joists with floorboards
   fixed both sides to adjust depth,
   and mineral wool insulation between
   40/60 mm battens
   vapour barrier
   60/80 mm channels
   15 mm plasterboard
6 ground floor construction:
   20 mm larch floorboards
   20 mm timber battens,
   with mineral wool insulation between
   22/20 mm mineral wool impact sound
   insulation
   vapour barrier
   22 mm chipboard
   120/80 mm timber joists,
   with 80 mm mineral wool insulation between
   bitumen waterproofing
   120 mm ground slab

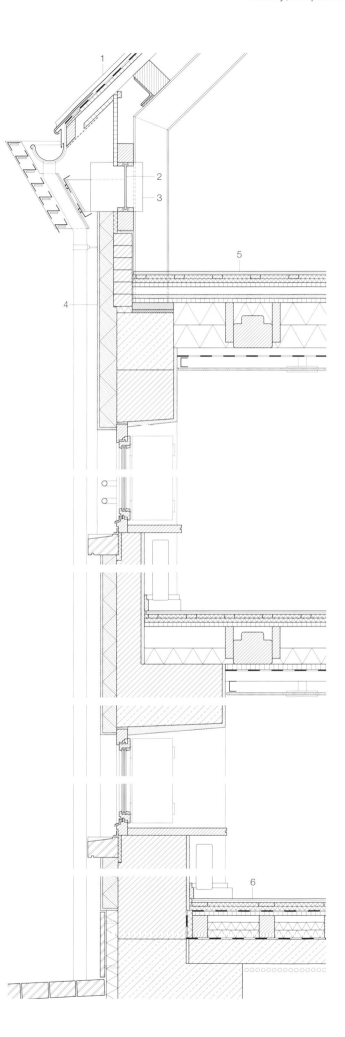

1   a   Ventilation system to upper floor
        (ground floor similar)
        In terms of the ventilation, the plan layout is di-
        vided into four zones each supplied by its own
        unit. As there is only one link between each of
        the four zones, sound transmission between the
        different areas is greatly reduced. The fresh-air
        ducts are laid above the suspended ceiling, the
        air inlets positioned above the windows. The air
        is extracted via the internal sanitary areas, thus
        achieving an optimum flow through the interior.
    b   Ventilation plant in roof space
        The four ventilation units are housed in two cab-
        inets which form the walls to the staircase to the

roof space. This arrangement means it is still
possible to divide up the roof space for ventilation purposes at a later date.
    c   Heat distribution and heat output
        Heat output is via tubular radiators mounted
        above the windows. As these radiators are all
        the same size, the flow temperature is dictated
        by the room with the highest heating require-
        ment. The regular positioning of the windows
        leads to an identical opening size related to the
        floor area of the room so that the solution cho-
        sen meets the architectural requirements and is
        also sensible from the heating point of view.

Active concept

Existing construction

Prior to refurbishment, the rectory was heated with an oil-fired boiler located on the ground floor. Hot water was provided via local electric heaters.

Refurbishment

The heating installation in the new parish hall also supplies the refurbished rectory. The LPG-fired condensing boiler is assisted by a solar energy system for both hot water and space heating. In order to cut the ventilation heat losses and to guarantee hygienic conditions, controlled ventilation with heat recovery was installed. Fresh air is drawn in at the ridge and exhaust air is emitted into the roof space, but escapes to the outside air thanks to the natural cross-ventilation of the roof space. The warm exhaust air leads to a noticeable temperature rise in the roof space, which in turn reduces the heat losses through the suspended floor structure forming the upper boundary to the heated upper floor of the building.

Verification

Verification according to the Energy Conservation Act in this case requires an elaborate energy performance analysis because the limiting values for the opaque external wall surfaces are exceeded in an assessment of individual values. In the energy performance analysis the limiting values for primary energy requirement Q_p and transmission heat losses H_T' through the enclosing surfaces may in each case be exceeded by 40% when the project involves an existing building.

When calculating the plant cost index, it should be remembered that the production losses of the heating plant must be related to the entire heated area, i.e. parish hall and rectory, whereas the distribution losses also include the connecting lines to the old rectory. This results in different installation losses for the new and refurbished buildings.

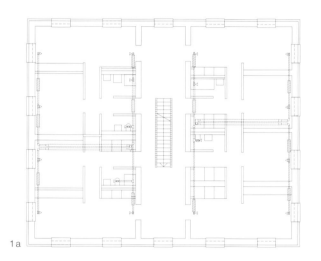

1a

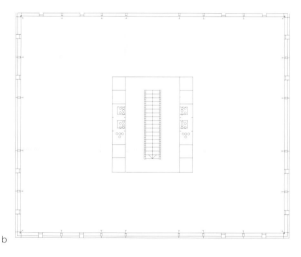

b

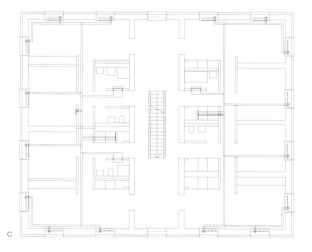

c

2 Installation (schematic)
   a LPG tank
   b Condensing boiler
   c Water tank
   d Buffer tank
   e Solar collectors
   f Ventilation with
      heat recovery
   g Heat output

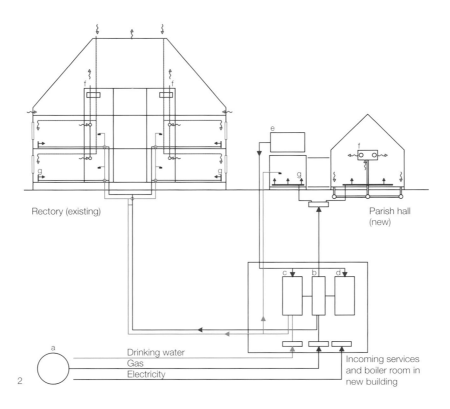

Rectory (existing)   Parish hall (new)

a

Drinking water
Gas
Electricity   Incoming services and boiler room in new building

2

Building data

	Existing building	Refurbished building
Basic data		
Energy reference area	500 m²	500 m²
Heated volume	2210 m³	2280 m³
Enclosing surface area	1160 m²	1200 m²
Volume of air	1500 m³	1450 m³
Air change rate	1	0.5
Passive concept		
Soil to unheated space	1.6 W/m²K	0.3 W/m²K
Wall	1.2 W/m²K	0.5 W/m²K
Suspended floor	1.0 W/m²K	0.2 W/m²K
Windows	2.8 W/m²K	1.4 W/m²K
g-value	0.8	0.7
Active concept		
Final energy		
Heating	200 kWh/m²a	80 kWh/m²a
Resource	oil	gas
Hot water	20 kWh/m²a	10 kWh/m²a
Resource	electricity	gas
Auxiliary energy		
Fans (ventilation)		5 kWh/m²a
Pumps	2 kWh/m²a	4 kWh/m²a
Ecology (according to GEMIS and DIN 4701-10)		
CO_2	75 kg CO_2/m²a	30 kg CO_2/m²a
Primary energy	286 kWh/m²a	126 kWh/m²a
Economy		
Energy cost-savings		3,000 €/year

Point-block, Ingolstadt

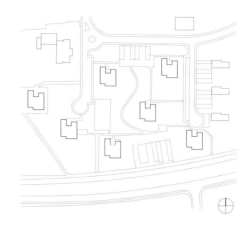

Architects: Adam Architekten, Munich
Engineers: Koch, Frey, Donaubauer, Ingolstadt
Building physics: GN Bauphysik, Stuttgart
Completion: 1968, 2003

Architecture

This nine-storey apartment block erected in 1968 is part of a housing complex consisting of seven separate, identical point-blocks. The characteristic feature of this heavyweight design is the differentiated arrangement of the structure, the facades and the internal access areas, which was developed from the half-storey offset of the apartment floors around the internal staircase.

The energy efficiency inadequacies were eliminated on all seven buildings successively according to the principle outlined here. One essential element in the measures was the glazed enclosure of the balconies, which has led to a considerable change in the external appearance.

Passive concept

Existing construction

The following inadequacies led to the decision to carry out a total refurbishment of the building envelope:

- high heat losses
- cracks in the upper storeys and subsequent saturation of the masonry
- damage to the cantilevering concrete balconies
- mould growth around the thermal bridges

Refurbishment

All apartments remained occupied during the work. There was no change to the plan layout; all the work was carried out outside the apartments. The installment of a thermal insulation composite system (120 mm thick) and new windows led to a considerable reduction in the heat losses through the building envelope. Additional safety barriers had to be provided in the new windows to comply with current regulations. Exterior roller shutters improved the quality of the apartments.

Another important aspect of the refurbishment project involved the balconies, which had to be repaired and protected

Building data

	Existing building	Refurbished building
Basic data		
Energy reference area	2580 m²	2580 m²
beheiztes Volumen	8800 m³	8800 m³
Heated volume	3100m²	3100m²
Volume of air	6200 m³	6200 m³
Air change rate	1	0.55
Passive concept		
Soil to unheated space	1.6 W/m²K	1.6 W/m²K
Wall	1.2 W/m²K	0.3 W/m²K
Roof	1.0 W/m²K	0.2 W/m²K
Windows	2.8 W/m²K	1.4 W/m²K
g-value	0.80	0.70
Active concept		
Final energy		
Heating	158 kWh/m²a	84 kWh/m²a
Source	district heating	district heating
Hot water	60 kWh/m²a	60 kWh/m²a
Source	district heating	district heating
Auxiliary energy		
Pumps	3 kWh/m²a	2 kWh/m²a
Fans (ventilation)	–	2 kWh/m²a
Ecology		
(to GEMIS and DIN 4701-10)		
CO_2	49 kg CO_2/m²a	34 kg CO_2/m²a
Primary energy	162 kWh/m²a	113 kWh/m²a
Economy		
Energy cost-savings		4,000 €/year

permanently against the weather by means of sliding glass elements. The sliding elements are mounted on steel supports that are anchored back to the structure with diagonal steel ties, which at the same time help to stabilise the existing concrete spandrel panels to the balconies. The single glazing which encloses the balcony creates a thermal buffer zone which raises the temperature of the continuous balcony slab in the winter to such an extent that the risk of mould growth in the interior is considerably reduced. Owing to this buffer effect, it was possible to retain the old windows facing onto the balconies – a major cost-saving. However, in summer intensive ventilation is required to prevent the balconies – now loggias – from generating additional heat loads.

Active concept

Existing construction
The housing complex is connected to a district heating system; there was no need to make any alterations with regard to the heating plant.

Refurbishment
Installing new windows and eliminating the thermal bridges at the balconies made it necessary to install a controlled extract system in order to avoid higher concentrations of moisture in the interior air (risk of mould growth). To do this, the existing ventilation ducts to the internal bathrooms were used and connected to a central fan in the topmost storey which ensures continuous extraction. Computer simulations revealed that the infiltration of the old balcony windows (which were retained) was sufficient to ensure an adequate supply of fresh air to replace the extracted air. The advantage of this during the colder months of the year is that the fresh air drawn in from the loggias is marginally warmer, but it requires that the occupants ventilate properly during the summer. Drawing in the air via the loggia also prevents moist interior air from condensing on the inside of the single-glazed sliding glass elements.

Verification

An assessment of the individual component values according to Appendix 3, Table 1 of the Energy Conservation Act shows that the requirements are met.

Location plan
scale 1:5000
Plan
scale 1:500
Vertical section
scale 1:20

1 roof construction, balcony:
   PUR roof panel, loadbearing
   40/60/4 mm steel channel framing
   40/80/3 mm steel RHS
2 sliding element, 12 mm toughened safety glass
3 wooden window (existing)
4 thermal insulation composite system:
   silicone resin decorative render, 3 mm aggregate
   5–10 mm mineral render undercoat
   100 mm thermal insulation
   150 mm masonry (existing)
   30 mm coated thermal insulation panels (existing)
5 40 mm bonded screed laid to fall (existing)

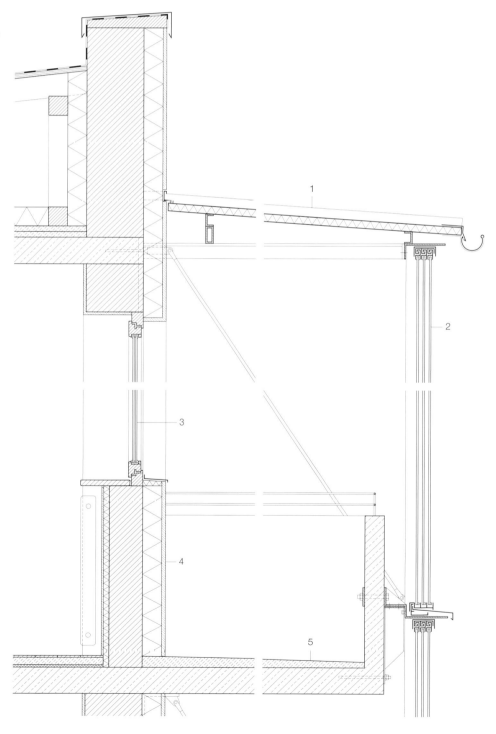

Prefabricated panel block, Leinefelde

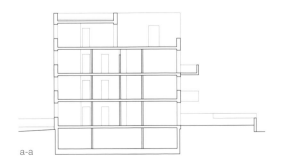

Architects: Stefan Forster Architekten,
Frankfurt am Main
Engineer: Gerhardt Rittmeier, Dingelstädt
Building physics: Hartlep & Höch, Leinefelde
Completion: 1961, 2004

Architecture

The conversion of this prefabricated
panel block in Leinefelde represents an
interesting example of sustainable refurbishment. Whereas new developments
among the existing building stock usually
concentrate on expansion options, in
Leinefelde the emphasis was on maintaining the existing fabric by reducing the
mass of the building. Formerly five and
six storeys high, the buildings on this
estate have been reduced to three- and
four-storey buildings with landscaped
internal courtyards. The example shown
here has been reduced to four storeys,
and the entrances, originally four facing
the road, have been replaced by two
accessed from the internal courtyard.
Each of the ground-floor apartments has
a small garden, each third floor apartment
a large rooftop terrace. The conversion
work resulted in a number of different
apartment layouts. For economic reasons,
the thermal performance requirements do
not exceed the statutory provisions.

Passive concept

Existing construction
The many prefabricated panel buildings
in former East Germany were built with a

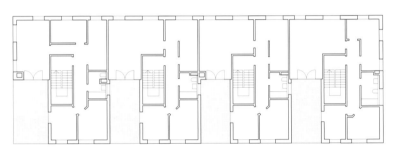

3rd floor

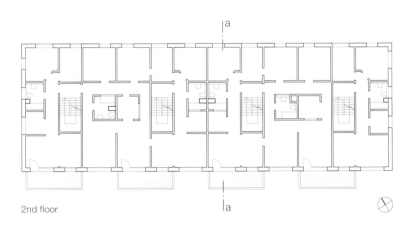

2nd floor

Plans, section
scale 1:400

a-a

94

Vertical section
scale 1:20

1   roof terrace:
    120/28 mm grid of pressure-impregnated larch
    50 mm grid supports on gravel
    2 x bitumen sheeting
    200 mm thermal insulation laid to fall
    vapour barrier
    150 mm reinforced concrete slab (existing)
2   2–3 mm render, synthetic resin
    100 mm thermal insulation
    140 x 140 mm timber framing with
    16 mm OSB to both sides
3   double-glazed window, plastic frame
    4 mm toughened safety glass + 16 mm cavity +
    4 mm toughened safety glass
4   2–3 mm render, synthetic resin
    100 mm thermal insulation

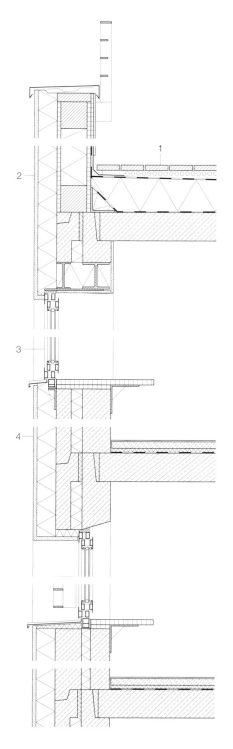

minimal thermal performance according to the valid GDR regulations of the time. That minimal thermal performance was defined in TGL 3420 – roughly equivalent to the minimum thermal performance requirements of DIN 4108.

Refurbishment
The refurbishment work included an energy-efficiency upgrade to meet the requirements of the Energy Conservation Act. A thermal insulation composite system with 100 mm insulation thickness was applied to the facades, the new windows have a U-value of 1.3 W/m²K and 200 mm of thermal insulation was laid on the roofs. The concrete walls and slabs of the old balconies were removed and replaced by new steel balconies repositioned to suit the new internal layout. The new balconies have a plain cladding and are anchored back to the structure with concealed fixings.

Active concept
Existing construction
The existing district heating system is characterised by an optimum layout (routed through the basement) and only minimal losses. This system covers both space heating and hot water requirements.

Refurbishment
The district heating system was overhauled during the refurbishment work and the flow temperature reduced to 90°C. However, the fundamental problem of district heating – the high distribution losses in summer – still remains. In power stations that are operated to meet electricity demands, such distribution losses are simply accepted because the heat cannot be avoided anyway. But in pure heating plants, optimising the installations can achieve a considerable reduction in the consumption of resources.

Verification
An assessment of the individual component values according to Appendix 3, Table 1 of the Energy Conservation Act is required, or the issuance of an energy requirement certificate, like for new buildings.
Owing to the extent of the measures (cl. 13), verification according to the Energy Conservation Act was carried out here using the energy performance method. The limiting values applicable for new buildings may therefore be exceeded by up to 40%. Maintaining the primary energy limiting value is no problem in this case because the district heating connection has a very favourable primary energy factor. And thanks to the new insulation to the external components, the transmission heat losses related to the area of the enclosing surfaces are also acceptable.

Building data

	Existing building	Refurbished building
Basic data		
Energy reference area	2740 m²	2285 m²
Heated volume	8710 m³	7140 m³
Enclosing surface area	2480 m²	2320 m²
Volume of air	6790 m³	5710 m³
Air change rate	1	0.7
Passive concept		
Soil to unheated space	1.6 W/m²K	0.38 W/m²K
Wall	1.2 W/m²K	0.3/0.5 W/m²K
Roof	1.0 W/m²K	0.34 W/m²K
Windows	2.8 W/m²K	1.30 W/m²K
g-value	0.80	0.70
Active concept		
Final energy		
Heating	200 kWh/m²a	80 kWh/m²a
Source	district heating	district heating
Hot water	60 kWh/m²a	60 kWh/m²a
Source	district heating	district heating
Auxiliary energy		
Pumps	4.0 kWh/m²a	3 kWh/m²a
Ecology		
(to GEMIS and DIN 4701-10)		
CO_2	59 kg CO_2/m²a	32 kg CO_2/m²a
Primary energy	194 kWh/m²a	107 kWh/m²a
Economy		
Energy cost-savings		1,000 €/year

Methods for assessing the energy balance

A sizeable assortment of regulations, directives and standards is now available to help us record, evaluate and optimise the energy performance of existing buildings. In Germany, the principal document is the Energy Conservation Directive, which was last revised in July 2005 to comply with additional European Union stipulations. The main revisions relate to the inclusion of HVAC installations and lighting systems in the energy performance assessment and the introduction of energy performance certificates for existing buildings. The Energy Conservation Act – the statutory instrument that expresses the objectives of the Energy Conservation Directive in practical terms by way of precise methods of analysis and verification – has been revised accordingly and presented to the bodies responsible for their comments and recommendations. A decision regarding the revised version is expected in early 2007.

Besides this statutory, precisely defined method for determining the energy requirement, there is also the "energy consulting" approach, which is not standardised and is subject to fewer regulations. Without the fixed boundary conditions of the Energy Conservation Act, this approach deals in more detail with the actual behaviour of the users of the respective building with the aim of drawing up and assessing optimisation measures.

Standards

The methods of calculation forming the basis for determining the relevant values for the energy requirements are not new developments devised especially for the Energy Conservation Act, but instead make use of the provisions of various existing DIN standards.

Energy Conservation Act reference standards

Standard	Edition	Title
DIN 4102-13	May 1990	Fire behaviour of building materials and elements; fire-resistant glazing; concepts, requirements and testing
DIN 4108 supplement 2	Jan 2004	Thermal insulation and energy economy in buildings – Thermal bridges Examples for planning and performance
DIN 4108-2	Jul 2003	Thermal protection and energy economy in buildings – Part 2: Minimum requirements for thermal insulation
DIN 4108-3	Jul 2001	Thermal insulation and energy economy in buildings – Part 3: Protection against moisture subject to climate conditions; requirements and directions for design and construction
DIN 4108-3 amendment 1	Apr 2004	Corrigenda to DIN 4108-3
DIN V 4108-4	Jul 2004	Thermal insulation and energy economy in buildings – Part 4: Characteristic values relating to thermal insulation and protection against moisture
DIN V 4108-6	Jun 2003	Thermal protection and energy economy in buildings – Part 6: Calculation of annual heat and energy use
DIN V 4108-6 amendment 1	Mar 2004	Corrigenda to DIN 4108-6
DIN 4108-7	Aug 2001	Thermal insulation and energy economy of buildings – Part 7: Airtightness of building, reqmt., recommendations and examples for planning and performance
DIN V 4108-10	Jun 2004	Thermal insulation and energy economy in buildings – Application related requirements for thermal insulation materials – Part 10: Factory-made products
DIN V 4701-10	Aug 2003	Energy efficiency of heating and ventilation systems in buildings – Part 10: Heating, domestic hot water, ventilation
DIN V 4701-10 supplement 1	Feb 2002	Energy efficiency of heating and ventilation systems in buildings – Part 10: Heating, domestic hot water, ventilation supplement 1: examples of systems
DIN V 4701-12	Feb 2004	Energetic evaluation of heating and ventilation systems in existing buildings – Part 12: Heat generation and domestic hot water generation
DIN V 18599-1 to 10	Jul 2005	Energy efficiency of buildings – Calculation of the net, final and primary energy demand for heating, cooling, ventilation, domestic hot water and lighting
DIN EN 410	Dec 1998	Glass in building – Determination of luminous and solar characteristics of glazing
DIN EN 673	Jun 2003	Glass in building – Determination of thermal transmittance (U-value) – Calculation method (including Amendment A1:2000 + Amendment A2:2002)
DIN EN 832	Jun 2003	Thermal performance of building – Calculation of energy use for heating – Residential buildings (includes Corrigenda AC:2002)
DIN EN 12207	Jun 2000	Windows and doors – Air permeability – Classification
DIN EN 13829	Feb 2001	Thermal performance of buildings – Determination of air permeability of buildings – Fan pressurization method (ISO 9972:1996, modified)
DIN EN ISO 717-1	Jan 1997	Acoustics – Rating of sound insulation in buildings and of building elements – Part 1: Airborne sound insulation (ISO 717-1:1996)
DIN EN ISO 6946	Nov 1996	Building components – Thermal resistance and thermal transmittance – Calculation method (ISO 6946:1996)
DIN EN ISO 6946	Oct 2003	Building components and building elements – Thermal resistance and thermal transmittance – Calculation method (ISO 6946:1996 + Amd 1:2003) (includes Amendment A1:2003)
DIN EN ISO 10077-1	Nov 2000	Thermal performance of windows, doors and shutters – Calculation of thermal transmittance – Part 1: General (ISO/DIS 10077-1:2004)
DIN EN ISO 10211-1	Nov 1995	Thermal bridges in building construction – Heat flows and surface temperatures – Part 1: General calculation methods (ISO 10211-1:1995)
DIN EN ISO 10211-2	Jun 2001	Thermal bridges in building construction – Calculation of heat flows and surface temperatures – Part 2: Linear thermal bridges (ISO 10211-2:2001)
DIN EN ISO 13370	Dec 1998	Thermal performance of buildings – Heat transfer via the ground – Calculation methods (ISO 13370:1998)
DIN EN ISO 13789	Oct 1999	Thermal performance of buildings – Transmission heat loss coefficient – Calculation method (ISO 13789:1999)
DIN EN ISO 13790	Sept 2004	Thermal performance of buildings – Calculation of energy use for space heating (ISO 13790:2004)

1

1   The Energy Conservation Act 2004 relies on methods for calculating the energy balance already prescribed in various DIN standards (plus: DIN V 18599).

German Energy Conservation Act 2004
Thermal performance in winter
The Energy Conservation Act calls for certain limit values to be observed regarding
- the specific transmission heat loss H_T' (in W/m²K) related to the heat-transferring enclosing surface area, and
- the annual primary energy requirement Q_p, which is either related to the heated volume of the building (Q_p' in kWh/m³a) or the usable floor area of the building (Q_p'' in kWh/m²a).

There are also conditions to be met regarding the imperviousness of the building, the minimum air change rate and the minimum thermal performance. The two limit values above depend on the so-called compactness of the respective building (A/V_e), its use (residential or non-residential), the window area proportion (> 30% or < 30%) and the hot-water provision (figure 2).
Whereas the average transmission heat loss H_T' related to the heat-transferring enclosing surface area depends exclu-

sively on the standard of thermal insulation of the building (essentially determined by the U-values of the individual components), the annual primary energy requirement Qp employs complex methods of calculation to take into account the following factors in addition to the transmission heat losses:
- energy losses due to ventilation,
- energy gains due to incoming solar radiation and internal heat sources (people, equipment),
- plant and installation losses, and
- the embedded energy in production and transportation of the energy sources required (oil, gas, electricity and others). Furthermore, the auxiliary energy required to operate heating installations (electricity for pumps) is also incorporated into the primary energy calculation (see also p. 56). The energy requirement for hot-water provision is determined using the same method as the primary energy requirement for the space heating.
Pre-standard DIN V 4108-6 stipulates two methods of calculation: the simplified

Energy Conservation Act requirements – appendix 1

| A/V_e | Annual primary energy requirement | | | Specific transmission heat loss related to heat-transferring enclosing surface area | |
| | Q_p'' [kWh/m²a] related to usable floor area of building | | Q_p' [kWh/m³a] related to heated volume of building | H_T' [W/m²K] | |
	Residential buildings except those according to column 3	Residential buildings with hot-water provision essentially by electricity	Other buildings	Non-residential buildings with a window area proportion ≤ 30% and residential bldgs.	Non-residential buildings with a window area proportion > 30%
≤ 0.2	66.00 + 2600/(100 + A_N)	88.00	14.72	1.05	1.55
0.3	73.53 + 2600/(100 + A_N)	95.53	17.13	0.80	1.15
0.4	81.06 + 2600/(100 + A_N)	103.06	19.54	0.68	0.95
0.5	88.58 + 2600/(100 + A_N)	110.58	21.95	0.60	0.83
0.6	96.11 + 2600/(100 + A_N)	118.11	24.36	0.55	0.75
0.7	103.64 + 2600/(100 + A_N)	125.64	26.77	0.51	0.69
0.8	111.17 + 2600/(100 + A_N)	133.17	29.18	0.49	0.65
0.9	118.70 + 2600/(100 + A_N)	140.70	31.59	0.47	0.62
1.0	126.23 + 2600/(100 + A_N)	148.23	34.00	0.45	0.59
≥1.05	130.00 + 2600/(100 + A_N)	152.00	35.21	0.44	0.58

2   Energy Conservation Act requirements for new buildings with normal internal temperatures (≥ 19°C): maximum values for annual primary energy requirement and specific transmission heat loss depending on compactness of building (A/V_e)

3 The primary energy requirement according to the Energy Conservation Act is calculated in a complex procedure based on the constructional and HVAC installation concepts. The heating requirement for hot water is included in the calculations according to defined boundary conditions.
4 The method of verification according to the Energy Conservation Act defines numerous parameters in order to be able to compare buildings irrespective of climate data and users' habits. Verification according to the Act therefore permits no conclusions to be made about the actual heating energy consumption.

heating period method for residential buildings with a window area ≤ 30%, and the more complicated monthly balance method, which can be used for all buildings with normal internal temperatures (≥ 19°C). A computer is required for the latter method, but it is more accurate and enables considerably better differentiated evaluations, which is particularly helpful when trying to optimise a building.
An elaborate analysis of the annual primary energy requirement Qp is not necessary for buildings with low internal temperatures (12–19°C). In such cases it is sufficient when the specific transmission heat loss H_T' does not exceed a certain specified limit value.

The results of the Energy Conservation Act analysis are recorded on the "energy performance certificate" according to cl. 13 of the Act. The certificate serves to assess the energy-related "quality" of a building in an abstract form, i.e. with specified boundary conditions. The main difference between the Energy Conservation Act and previous statutory instruments covering thermal performance is that both passive (constructional measures) and active (installation measures) concepts are considered simultaneously and the energy requirement for hot-water provision is also included (see also fig. 4, p. 8).
In contrast to the looser concept of "energy consulting", climate data and factors related to the use of the building, e.g. room temperature, ventilation heat losses, internal heat gains or actual hot-water consumption, are defined by fixed variables. The outcome of the calculation is therefore a building assessment that is not dependent on users' behaviour and thus enables a comparison with any similar buildings throughout the country.

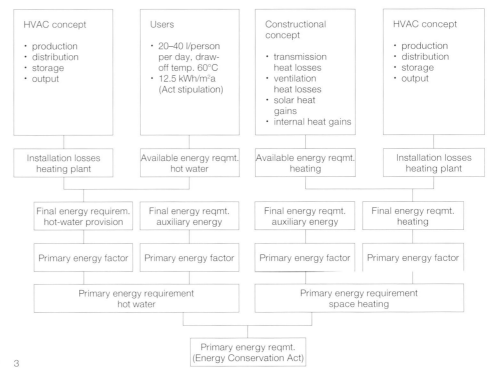

3

Energy Conservation Act verification method – defined parameters

Parameter	Act (monthly balance method)	Remarks
Energy reference area	$0.32 \times V_e$	The global value assumed is usually higher than the actual usable conditioned floor area (V_e = heated gross volume).
Energy reference area	$0.76 \times V_e$ or $0.8 \cdot V_e$	The higher value applies to buildings with more than three proper stories.
Internal temperature	19°C	Average internal temperature of all rooms during heating period.
Internal heat gains	5 W/m²	
Air change rate	0.7/h or 0.6/h	Lower value appl. for verif. of imperviousness
Thermal bridges surcharge	0.1 W/m²K or 0.05 W/m²K	The lower value applies for calculations as set forth in DIN 4108 supp. 2.
Incoming solar radiation factor (window area)	0.567	Reduction factor for frame component, soiling, shading caused by reveal.
Climate	Germany	Würzburg is the reference location for Germany.
Hot water heating reqirem.	12.5 kWh/m²	Heating requirement without installation losses.
Sunshading	0.25 to 1	Reduction factors from DIN 4108-2 tab. 8.
HVAC installation	Tabular values as set forth in DIN 4701-10	Simplified assessment of production, distribution, storage and output losses.

4

Thermal performance in summer
This aspect, i.e. protection against overheating in summer (the importance of which is frequently underestimated), is treated in much more detail in the new Act. Verification of compliance with the Act is required for all buildings whose window area proportion (related to the area of the facade) is > 30%. To do this, a permissible maximum value is calculated first depending on the climate region, the ventilation options of the building and the heat storage capacity of its components. This value may not be exceeded in the areas of the building with the highest summertime heat gains, which can usually be achieved through corresponding sunshading measures (coatings on the glass or additional components), but in less favourable situations may require reducing in the size of the windows, improving to the storage capacity or installing of a mechanical cooling system.

It should also be noted that the minimum summertime thermal performance standard specified in DIN 4108-2 is higher than the target values of the Energy Conservation Act. According to the DIN standard, an analysis of the thermal performance in summer is required for a window area proportion ≥ 10% (related to the floor area of the room) and not just for a window area proportion of ≥ 30% related to the total area of the facade (see p. 50).

Refurbishment
Whereas all new buildings with normal internal temperatures must be analysed in accordance with the Act, different stipulations and methods of calculation apply to measures in existing buildings depending on their extent. These are specified in cl. 8 and appendix 3 (constructional measures) and cl. 9 (HVAC installations) of the Energy Conservation Act.

For refurbishment measures that involve more than 20% of the area of the building envelope facing in one direction, it is generally sufficient to ensure that the components involved comply with certain specified U-values (figure 5).

As an alternative to this analysis of individual values, the Energy Conservation Act permits an overall energy performance analysis in which the permissible maximum values for H_T' and Q_p may be exceeded by 40% (figure 6).

Whereas an analysis of individual values is advisable for individual refurbishment measures such as insulating the facade or replacing the windows, an overall energy performance analysis is recom-

Energy Conservation Act requirements, verification of individual component values for refurbishment

Component	adjacent to...	U-value	Remarks
Wall	outside air	0.45	
	outside air	0.35	Where thermal insulation is being installed for the first time or for a wall with U > 0.9 W/m²K whose render/plaster is being renewed.
	unheated	0.5	When installing thermal insulation layers
	soil	0.5	When installing thermal insulation layers
Window	outside air	1.7	When installing new windows ($U_{w, BW}$)
Glazing	outside air	1.5	When replacing the glazing (U_g) (different values for special glazing types)
Floor	unheated	0.5	When installing thermal insulation layers
	soil	0.5	When installing thermal insulation layers
Pitched roof	outside air	0.3	When renewing roof covering
Flat roof	outside air	0.25	When renewing roof covering

5   Energy Conservation Act requirements with respect to the verification of individual component values according to cl. 8 (1) for refurbishment measures: maximum U-values in W/m²K for first fitment, replacement and renewal of components in buildings with normal internal temperatures (≥ 19°C). 5

mended for more extensive refurbishment projects involving various constructional measures and possibly also changes to the installations.

If when assessing the overall energy performance the data of an existing, old heating installation (which is to be retained) cannot be determined exactly, it is not necessary to verify the primary energy requirement. Instead, only HT' needs to be assessed, but then the 40% allowance must be reduced by 24% (cl. 3) (figure 7).

If several refurbishment measures – including changes to the heating installation – are carried out in a building within one year, a detailed investigation is required to assess whether this constitutes a "substantial modification" according to cl. 13 (2), which would then require a complete energy performance analysis.

Extensions

If an existing building is extended, the procedure depends on the size of the extension.

There are no requirements – apart from minimum thermal performance to DIN 4108-2 – to be satisfied if the extension is <30 m³ (heated volume). For extensions measuring 30–100 m³, the new components merely have to comply with the requirements of appendix 3, i.e. the same limit values for thermal transmittance as for a refurbishment (cl. 7). In the case of extensions >100 m³, an energy performance certificate is required as for a new building. Here again, it may be the case that the new extension is served by an existing heating installation, the data of which is unknown. In such cases, an analysis of the primary energy requirement is not required, but then the permissible H_T' value must be reduced by 24% according to cl. 3.

If an existing building is refurbished and also extended, e.g. a roof space conver-

sion, the two projects must be treated separately.

However, if the heated volume of the building is extended by more than 50%, a complete analysis for the entire volume of the building is required according to cl. 13 (2).

6 Energy Conservation Act requirements for the total energy performance method when refurbishing residential buildings and including an assessment of the heating installation: permissible maximum values for specific transmission heat loss H_T' in W/m²K and annual primary energy requirement Q_p'' in kWh/m²a related to usable floor area of building may be 40% higher than for new buildings (cl. 8 (2) of Act).

7 Energy Conservation Act requirements for the total energy performance method when refurbishing residential buildings but not including the heating installation owing to lack of appropriate data: verification of annual primary energy requirement is not required, but instead the permissible maximum value for H_T' in W/m²K must be reduced by 24% (cl. 3 (3) of Act).

Energy Conservation Act requirements for total energy performance method for refurbishment work including assessment of heating installation

A/V$_e$	H_T' new building (see fig. 2)	H_T' refurbishment (plus 40% acc. to cl. 8)	Q_p'' new building (see fig. 2)	Q_p'' refurbishment (plus 40% to cl. 8)
0.20	1.05	1.47	68.00	95.20
0.30	0.80	1.12	75.53	105.74
0.40	0.68	0.95	83.06	116.28
0.50	0.60	0.84	90.58	126.81
0.60	0.55	0.77	98.11	137.35
0.70	0.51	0.71	105.64	147.90
0.80	0.49	0.69	113.70	159.18
0.90	0.47	0.66	120.70	168.98
1.00	0.45	0.63	128.23	179.52
> 1.05	0.44	0.62	132.00	184.80

6 Q_p'' is given here for a residential building with 1200 m² usable floor area (example)

Energy Conservation Act requirements for total energy performance method for refurbishment work excluding assessment of heating installation

A/V$_e$	H_T' new building (see fig. 2)	H_T' refurbishment (plus 40% acc. to cl. 8)	H_T' refurbishment without installation (minus 24% acc. to cl. 3)
0.20	1.05	1.47	1.12
0.30	0.80	1.12	0.85
0.40	0.68	0.95	0.72
0.50	0.60	0.84	0.64
0.60	0.55	0.77	0.59
0.70	0.51	0.71	0.54
0.80	0.49	0.69	0.52
0.90	0.47	0.66	0.50
1.00	0.45	0.63	0.48
> 1.05	0.44	0.62	0.47

7

Revised German Energy Conservation Act 2006/2007 (draft)

EU directive

According to article 7 of EU directive 2002/91/EC, every building requires an energy performance certificate. Such a certificate is compulsory not only for new buildings, but also when (re-)letting and selling existing buildings and residential property.

The aim of the energy performance certificate is to make the owners or users of a building aware of its energy performance and thus foster a demand for energy-efficient buildings. A certificate must be easy for the layman to understand and should include reference values such as current legal standards and benchmarks to enable comparisons and assessments regarding the energy performance of the building, as well as recommendations for the cost-effective improvement of the energy performance. EU member states are obliged to incorporate this directive into their national laws by January 2006; however, an extension of up to three years is possible. The methods for calculating the energy performance of buildings should be based on the stipulations of the EU directive, but will be specified on a national or regional level by the member states themselves.

By the time this book went to press, the corresponding revision of the German Energy Conservation Act was only available in reference draft form. It will probably be published in early 2007 and will come into force in stages.

Pre-standard DIN V 18599

The new method contained in DIN V 18599, which was published as a pre-standard in 2005, will form the basis for the evaluation of energy performance in existing and new non-residential buildings when the revised edition of the Energy Conservation Act comes into force. The medium-term objective is for the new DIN standard to replace the thermal performance standards hitherto applicable for residential buildings as well, in particular DIN V 4108-6 (June 2003).

The energy performance evaluation of buildings according to DIN V 18599 is essentially much more comprehensive than in the past. Chiller plants, ventilation systems and lighting installations are also included in the assessment as well as a detailed evaluation of the heating installation.

Another difference to DIN V 4108-6 is the reference area used: the usable floor area is no longer calculated by multiplying the heated volume by the global factor of 0.32; instead, the true conditioned usable floor area is entered into the calculation. That makes the data acquisition considerably more involved, but leads to more realistic, better differentiated results. Large buildings with different uses are therefore divided into different zones (multi-zone model) which are then treated like individual buildings.

The differentiated approach of DIN V 18599 taking into account all relevant energy flows (heating, ventilation, cooling and lighting) has generally been greeted positively by the experts. However, the actual computational work required to divide up, for example, unimportant energy losses in the installations among the different zones is totally disproportionate to the knowledge gained thereby.

Method of analysis

When the revised Energy Conservation Act comes into force, residential and non-residential buildings will be assessed in different ways.

Whereas the method currently stipulated in the Energy Conservation Act 2004 will remain virtually unchanged with regard to refurbishment and extension work on residential buildings, the procedure for assessing the energy performance of non-residential buildings is totally new. This is because the method is based on DIN V 18599, which records and evaluates all energy consumption figures (heating, cooling, ventilation and lighting). The method of analysis comprises the following steps:

Firstly, calculate the target values H_T' and Q_p'' using a reference building. If there are different energy requirements within a building, e.g. the lighting of offices and shops within one block, form zones so that the energy balances of these different areas can be treated separately. The value for the total building is then worked out at the end of this process.

The method for assessing the energy performance is the same as in the Energy Conservation Act 2004 (currently valid). The requirements are determined based on the constructional concept and the type of usage, and evaluated in primary energy terms via the installations required to cover the requirements.

Energy performance certificate
One important revision to the Energy Conservation Act 2006/2007 concerns the introduction of energy performance certificates as required for all buildings by the EU directive. The new certificates will replace the "energy requirement certificates" issued in the past which show the results of the Energy Conservation Act assessment. For existing buildings, the new certificates will replace the "energy passes" which had been issued by the German Energy Agency (DEnA) in anticipation of an Energy Conservation Act revision.

From the above description of the method of analysis, we can see that there will be different energy performance certificates for residential and non-residential buildings. On the certificates a distinction

will be made between new building, existing building with modernisation measures or existing building requiring a certificate because of the impending (re-)letting or sale.

The debate surrounding the reference draft focuses on the proposed allowable options for existing buildings in the case of (re-)letting or sale, i.e. whether the data for the energy performance assessment should be calculated using standardised boundary conditions or the actual consumption.

The consumption-based energy performance certificate is easy to draw up and

therefore less expensive. It evaluates the ancillary costs data, which is available anyway, and is therefore based on the actual consumption, which is very much dependent on users' habits. However, this approach permits neither objective statements regarding the energy-related standard of the building nor sound recommendations for improvement measures. This method is especially questionable in the case of non-residential buildings because the energy consumption figures frequently contain items that do not belong in the audit but owing to the lack of separate measurements cannot

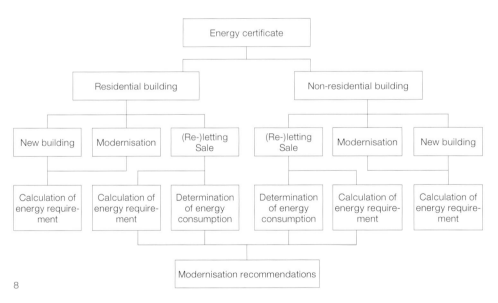

8

ENERGIEAUSWEIS für Wohngebäude
gemäß den §§ 16 ff. Energieeinsparverordnung (1)

Gültig bis:

Gebäude

Gebäudetyp	
Adresse	
Gebäudeteil	
Baujahr Gebäude	Gebäudefoto (freiwillig)
Baujahr Anlagentechnik	
Anzahl Wohnungen	
Gebäudenutzfläche (A_N)	

Anlass der Ausstellung des Energieausweises: ☐ Neubau ☐ Modernisierung ☐ Sonstiges (freiwillig) ☐ Vermietung / Verkauf (Änderung / Erweiterung)

Hinweise zu den Angaben über die energetische Qualität des Gebäudes

Die energetische Qualität eines Gebäudes kann durch die Berechnung des Energiebedarfs unter standardisierten Randbedingungen oder durch die Auswertung des Energieverbrauchs ermittelt werden. Als Bezugsfläche dient die energetische Gebäudenutzfläche nach der EnEV, die sich in der Regel von den allgemeinen Wohnflächenangaben unterscheidet. Die angegebenen Vergleichswerte sollen überschlägige Vergleiche ermöglichen (Erläuterungen – siehe Seite 4).

☐ Der Energieausweis wurde auf der Grundlage von Berechnungen des Energiebedarfs erstellt. Die Ergebnisse sind auf Seite 2 dargestellt. Diese Art der Ausstellung ist Pflicht bei Neubauten und bestimmten Modernisierungen. Zusätzliche Informationen zum Verbrauch sind freiwillig.

☐ Der Energieausweis wurde auf der Grundlage von Auswertungen des Energieverbrauchs erstellt. Die Ergebnisse sind auf Seite 3 dargestellt.

Datenerhebung Bedarf/Verbrauch durch ☐ Eigentümer ☐ Aussteller

☐ Dem Energieausweis sind zusätzliche Informationen zur energetischen Qualität beigefügt (freiwillige Angabe).

Hinweise zur Verwendung des Energieausweises

Der Energieausweis dient lediglich der Information. Die Angaben im Energieausweis beziehen sich auf das gesamte Wohngebäude oder den oben bezeichneten Gebäudeteil. Der Energieausweis ist lediglich dafür gedacht, einen überschlägigen Vergleich von Gebäuden zu ermöglichen.

Aussteller   Unterschrift des Ausstellers

Datum   Unterschrift

9a

ENERGIEAUSWEIS für Wohngebäude
gemäß den §§ 16 ff. Energieeinsparverordnung (2)

Berechneter Energiebedarf des Gebäudes

Energiebedarf

Primärenergiebedarf „Gesamtenergieeffizienz"
kWh/(m²·a)

0 50 100 150 200 250 300 350 400 >400

kWh/(m²·a)

Endenergiebedarf CO_2-Emissionen *   kg/(m²·a)

Nachweis der Einhaltung des § 3 oder § 9 Abs. 1 der EnEV (Vergleichswerte)

Primärenergiebedarf		Energetische Qualität der Gebäudehülle	
Gebäude Ist-Wert	kWh/(m²·a)	Gebäude Ist-Wert H_T'	W/(m²·K)
EnEV-Anforderungs-Wert	kWh/(m²·a)	EnEV-Anforderungs-Wert H_T'	W/(m²·K)

Endenergiebedarf „Normverbrauch"

Energieträger	Jährlicher Endenergiebedarf in kWh/(m²·a) für			Gesamt in kWh/(m²·a)
	Heizung	Warmwasser	Hilfsgeräte	

Erneuerbare Energien

Einsatzbarkeit alternativer Energieversorgungssysteme nach § 5 EnEV vor Baubeginn berücksichtigt:

Erneuerbare Energieträger werden genutzt für:
☐ Heizung ☐ Warmwasser
☐ Lüftung ☐ Kühlung

Lüftungskonzept
Die Lüftung erfolgt durch:
☐ Fensterlüftung ☐ Schachtlüftung
☐ Lüftungsanlage ohne Wärmerückgewinnung
☐ Lüftungsanlage mit Wärmerückgewinnung

Vergleichswerte Endenergiebedarf

0 50 100 150 200 250 300 400 >400

Erläuterungen zum Berechnungsverfahren

Das verwendete Berechnungsverfahren ist durch die EnEV vorgegeben. Insbesondere wegen standardisierter Randbedingungen erlauben die angegebenen Werte keine Rückschlüsse auf den tatsächlichen Energieverbrauch. Die ausgewiesenen Bedarfswerte sind spezifische Werte nach der EnEV pro Quadratmeter Gebäudenutzfläche (A_N).

* freiwillige Angabe ** EFH – Einfamilienhäuser, MFH – Mehrfamilienhäuser

b

ENERGIEAUSWEIS für Wohngebäude
gemäß den §§ 16 ff. Energieeinsparverordnung (3)

Gemessener Energieverbrauch des Gebäudes

Energieverbrauchskennwert

Dieses Gebäude:
kWh/(m²·a)

0 50 100 150 200 250 300 350 400 >400

Warmwasserverbrauch: ☐ enthalten ☐ nicht enthalten

Verbrauchserfassung – Heizung und Warmwasser

Energieträger	Abrechnungszeitraum		Brennstoff-menge [kWh]	Anteil Warm-wasser [kWh]	Klima-faktor	Energieverbrauchskennwert in kWh/(m²·a) (zeitlich bereinigt, klimabereinigt)			Kennwert
	von	bis				Heizung	Heizung einschl. Sicherheits-zuschlag	Warm-wasser	

Durchschnitt

Vergleichswerte Endenergiebedarf

0 50 100 150 200 250 300 400 >400

Die modellhaft ermittelten Vergleichswerte beziehen sich auf Gebäude, in denen die Wärme für Heizung und Warmwasser durch Heizkessel im Gebäude bereitgestellt wird. Soll ein Energieverbrauchskennwert verglichen werden, der keinen Warmwasseranteil enthält, ist zu beachten, dass auf die Warmwasserbereitung je nach Gebäudegröße 20 – 40 kWh/(m²·a) entfallen können. Soll ein Energieverbrauchskennwert eines mit Fern- oder Nahwärme beheizten Gebäudes verglichen werden, ist zu beachten, dass hier normalerweise ein um 15 – 30 % geringerer Energieverbrauch als bei vergleichbaren Gebäuden mit Kesselheizung zu erwarten ist.

Erläuterungen zum Verfahren

Das Verfahren zur Ermittlung von Energieverbrauchskennwerten ist durch die Energieeinsparverordnung vorgegeben. Insbesondere wegen standardisierter Randbedingungen erlauben die angegebenen Werte keine Rückschlüsse auf den tatsächlichen Energieverbrauch. Die Werte sind spezifische Werte pro Quadratmeter Gebäudenutzfläche (A_N) nach der EnEV.

* EFH – Einfamilienhäuser, MFH – Mehrfamilienhäuser

c

9 Revised Energy Conservation Act 2006/2007 (draft)
Energy certificate for residential buildings
a cover sheet (general information)
b calculated energy requirement
c measured energy consumption

be eliminated, e.g. electricity consumption for lifts or IT equipment. In such cases an evaluation by similar buildings is necessary.

On the face of it, the purely consumption-related energy performance certificate would satisfy the EU directive very simply and cost-effectively, but in the end it would not be particularly telling because a truly sustainable refurbishment requires a precise, individual analysis of the property.

Such an analysis will probably need a requirements-based energy performance certificate because this is based on the much more differentiated auditing method of the Energy Conservation Act. Using this approach, the property owner obtains an assessment of his property that provides a firm foundation for developing individual, coordinated refurbishment measures with permanent energy-savings. Of course, owing to its more detailed, more useful content, the cost of a requirements-based energy performance certificate is much higher than that of a consumption-based certificate, and should be based on cl. 78 of the HOAI (German scale of fees for architects and engineers).

The Act will regulate who is authorised to issue energy performance certificates and how the certificates will be checked, and according to the current status of the discussion will be identical throughout the country:

• Registered architects will be the only persons authorised to issue the full range of energy performance certificates.

• University graduates of architecture, civil/structural engineering, building services, building performance, mechanical engineering or electrical engineering will also be authorised to issue certificates provided they have completed defined training courses.

• Tradesman, technicians and interior architects will only be permitted to issue energy performance certificates for residential buildings; however, there are no plans to make this authorisation dependent on the size of the building.

The revised edition of the Energy Conservation Act will come into force in January 2007 at the very latest. The issuance of energy performance certificates for existing buildings upon (re-)letting or sale will not become mandatory until after the expiry of a transitional period. This period will be six months for residential buildings built up until 1965, 18 months for newer buildings, and 24 months for non-residential buildings.

Energy consulting

"Energy consulting" is not yet a defined term based on standardised procedures with reliable standards of quality and consultants with verifiable qualifications even though the term covers a range of tasks offering great potential.

In situ energy consulting

The cost of energy consulting as an independent method is subsidised in Germany by the Federal Office of Economics & Export Control (BAFA) as part of the programme for obtaining energy-saving

ENERGIEAUSWEIS für Nichtwohngebäude
gemäß den §§ 16 ff. Energieeinsparverordnung

Berechneter Energiebedarf des Gebäudes (2)

Primärenergiebedarf „Gesamtenergieeffizienz"
Dieses Gebäude:
kWh/(m²·a)
0 100 200 300 400 500 600 700 800 900 1000 >1000
EnEV-Anforderungswert Neubau | EnEV-Anforderungswert modernisierter Altbau | CO₂-Emissionen * kg/(m²·a)

Nachweis der Einhaltung des § 3 oder § 9 Abs. 1 der EnEV (Vergleichswerte)

Endenergiebedarf „Normverbrauch"

Aufteilung Energiebedarf

Erneuerbare Energien / Gebäudezonen

Lüftungskonzept

Erläuterungen zum Berechnungsverfahren

10a

ENERGIEAUSWEIS für Nichtwohngebäude
gemäß den §§ 16 ff. Energieeinsparverordnung

Gemessener Energieverbrauch des Gebäudes (3)

Heizenergieverbrauchskennwert (einschließlich Warmwasser)
Dieses Gebäude:
kWh/(m²·a)
0 100 200 300 400 500 600 700 800 900 1000 >1000

Stromverbrauchskennwert
Dieses Gebäude:
kWh/(m²·a)
0 100 200 300 400 500 600 700 800 900 1000 >1000

Verbrauchserfassung – Heizung und Warmwasser

Verbrauchserfassung – Strom / Gebäudekategorie

b

Modernisierungsempfehlungen zum Energieausweis
gemäß § 20 Energieeinsparverordnung

Gebäude

Empfohlene Modernisierungsmaßnahmen

Beispielhafter Variantenvergleich

11

advice. The intention is that property owners should have the energy performance qualities of their property explained and be given advice as to how each building can be improved in terms of its energy performance. The economic viability of the proposed energy-saving measures, which should also include the use of renewable energies, should be assessed by way of a costs/benefits analysis. Such energy consulting will also include advice on public grants and subsidies available to encourage investment in improving the use of energy.

Energy consultants should have undergone training recognised by BAFA or be able to prove their qualifications in some other way.

Energy consulting methods
It is advisable for energy consulting to be based on verification according to the Energy Conservation Act. In contrast to the Act, which aims to secure the best possible building standards in terms of energy performance using defined values which eliminate the need to consider the habits of individual users, energy consultants can choose any parameters (internal temperature, ventilation habits, water consumption, climate data, etc.) to assess each individual case realistically, analyse the energy consumption figures measured and, based on the results, target decisions regarding refurbishment recommendations.

Energy consulting means, firstly, analysing and recording the constructional circumstances (transmission heat losses, solar heat gains), then investigating

users' habits (internal gains, ventilation losses), and, finally, estimating the efficiency of the heating and hot-water installations. The resulting heating energy requirement in kilowatt-hours is converted into litres of oil or cubic metres of gas and compared with the actual consumption. If the figures do not correspond, all the influencing factors are investigated once again and adjusted accordingly until the computational model describes the real situation accurately and permits conclusions regarding the most serious weaknesses in terms of energy performance. Following this energy performance analysis, a catalogue of measures for saving energy is drawn up and the measures assessed in terms of costs and energy performance benefits. The scope and nature of the measures depend on the targets to be achieved as agreed with the property owner in advance. The constructional feasibility and the effects of the measures on the architecture of the building should not be forgotten. Recommendations and calculations regarding public grants and subsidies round off the package of services that make up energy consulting. As such grants and subsidies frequently refer to the values of the Energy Conservation Act, it is therefore advisable for any energy consulting work to be based on the methods of the Act.

In order to be able to assess and solve the complex nature of energy performance as a whole, the assistance of a correspondingly qualified architect will be indispensable.

The hope is that owing to the increasing demand for energy-efficient buildings

based on sustainable concepts, property owners will turn to energy consultants more and more in order to reach sound refurbishment decisions.

10 Revised Energy Conservation Act 2006/2007 (draft)
    EEnergy certificate for non-residential buildings
    a calculated energy requirement
    b measured energy consumption
11 Revised Energy Conservation Act 2006/2007 (draft)
    Modernisation recommendations as an appendix to the energy certificate for residential and non-residential buildings

Units of measurement

In the course of the ongoing developments and harmonisation among European and international standards, it is possible to encounter different terms and designations for the same concept. For example, the heating requirement for hot-water provision is given the suffix "w" in DIN 4108-6[1] but "tw" in pre-standard DIN V 4701-10[1]. The table on the right therefore does not claim to be exhaustive and lists only the principal variables necessary for understanding the Energy Conservation Act. All designations will change fundamentally once DIN V 18599 comes into force. For example, DIN V 18599 does not use the term heating energy requirement, but instead speaks of heat sinks (Q_{sink}) and heat sources (Q_{source}). And as the old designations will undoubtedly be retained at first, further confusion will be unavoidable.

[1] German standard

The complexity of the suffix allocation for various energy flows becomes clear when we take the installation variables from DIN V 4701-10 as an example:

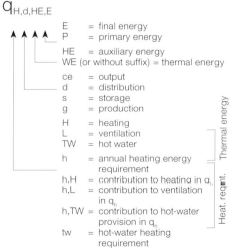

$q_{H,d,HE,E}$

E = final energy
P = primary energy
HE = auxiliary energy
WE (or without suffix) = thermal energy
ce = output
d = distribution
s = storage
g = production
H = heating
L = ventilation
TW = hot water
h = annual heating energy requirement
h,H = contribution to heating in q_h
h,L = contribution to ventilation in q_h
h,TW = contribution to hot-water provision in q_h
tw = hot-water heating requirement

Terms, symbols and units of measurement relevant to thermal performance (selection)

Term	Old symbol	New symbol	Unit	Source
Air change rate		n	h^{-1}	DIN V 4108-6, DIN 4108-7
Annual heating energy requirement		Q_h	kWh/a	DIN V 4701-10
Annual primary energy requirement (related to usable floor area)		Q_p''	kWh/m²a	DIN V 4701-10, E. C. Act
Annual primary energy requirement (related to volume)		Q_p'	kWh/m³a	DIN V 4701-10, E. C. Act
Area, usable floor area ($A_N = 0.32 \times V_e$)		A_N	m²	DIN V 4108-6
Area, enclosing surface area		A	m²	DIN EN ISO 7345, DIN 4108-2
Area-related quantity of energy per year		q	kWh/m²a	DIN V 4701-10
Building volume (related to external dimensions, gross)		V_e	m³	DIN EN ISO 7345, DIN 4108-2
Degree-day factor		F_{GT}	–	E. C. Act
Density		ρ	kg/m³	DIN EN ISO 7345, DIN 4108-2
Effective heat storage capacity	–	C_{wirk_h}	Wh/K	DIN V 4108-6
Energy		Q	kWh/a	DIN V 4701-10
Heat capacity of a component		C	Wh/K	DIN 4108-6
Heat, quantity of heat	Q	Q	kWh	DIN EN ISO 7345
Heat flux	Q'	φ		DIN 4108-2, DIN EN ISO 7345
Heat flux density	q	q		DIN 4108-2, DIN EN ISO 7345
Heat gain due to ventilation heat recovery system	–	Q_{WR}	kWh	DIN V 4108-6
Heating energy requirement (related to floor area)		Q_h''	kWh/m²a	DIN V 4108-6
Heating energy requirement (related to volume)		Q_h'	kWh/m³a	DIN V 4108-6
Joint permeability coefficient		a	–	DIN 4108-2
Linear thermal transmittance (thermal bridges loss coefficient)		ψ	W/mK	DIN 4108-6
Mass		m	kg	DIN EN ISO 7345, DIN 4108-2
Plant cost index		e_p	–	DIN V 4701-10
Primary energy conversion factor		f_p	–	DIN V 4701-10
Relative humidity (of air)	φ	φ	–	DIN 4108-2, DIN EN ISO 9346
Solar gain index		S	–	DIN 4108-2
Specific heat capacity		c	Wh/kgK	DIN 4108-6
Sunshading reduction factor		F_c	–	DIN 4108-2, DIN EN 832
Surface resistance, external	$1/\alpha_a$	R_{se}	m²K/W	DIN EN ISO 6946, DIN 4108-2
Surface resistance, internal	$1/\alpha_i$	R_{si}	m²K/W	DIN EN ISO 6946, DIN 4108-2
Temperature		ϑ	°C	DIN V 4701-10
Temperature (celsius)		Θ	°C	DIN EN ISO 7345, DIN 4108-2
Temperature correction for component x		F_x	–	DIN V 4108-6, E. C. Act
Temperature difference		Δϑ	K	DIN V 4701-10
Temperature factor		f_{Rsi}	–	DIN 4108-2
Thermal conductivity	λ	λ	W/mK	DIN EN 7345, DIN 4108-2
Thermal conductivity coefficient	Λ	Λ	W/m²K	DIN EN ISO 7345, DIN 4108-2
Thermal resistance	1/Λ	R	m²K/W	DIN EN ISO 7345, DIN 4108-2
Thermal transmittance	k	U	W/m²K	DIN EN 7345, DIN 4108-2
Thickness		d	m	DIN EN ISO 6946
Time	t	t	h, min, sec	DIN EN ISO 7345
Total energy transmittance		g	–	DIN 4108-2
Total thermal resistance	1/k	R_T	m²K/W	DIN EN ISO 6946
Transmission heat loss coefficient, specific		H_T	W/m²K	DIN EN ISO 13 789, app. B
Transmission heat loss coefficient, specific, related to heat-transferring enclosing surface area		H_T'	W/m²K	E. C. Act, appendix 1
Ventilation heat loss, specific		H_V	W/K	DIN V 4108-6, DIN EN 832
Window area proportion		f	–	DIN 4108-2

Upgrading incentives in Germany

Energy-efficiency upgrades are encouraged in various ways. In Germany, in addition to nationwide projects, assistance in the form of cheaper credit is available on a regional and even a local level and is frequently accompanied by direct subsidies for the respective matters. Furthermore, some power supply companies provide assistance in converting to different energy sources.

KfW – Kreditanstalt für Wiederaufbau
Applications:
KfW Förderbank
Palmengartenstraße 5–9
60325 Frankfurt am Main
Germany
Tel.:   +49 1801 33 55 77
or   +49 69 7431-0
Fax: +49 69 7431-2888
E-Mail: info@kfw.de
Internet: www.kfw-foerderbank.de/
EN_Home/index.jsp

BAFA – Bundesamt für Wirtschaft & Ausfuhrkontrolle
(Federal Office of Economics & Export Control)
Applications:
Bundesamt f. Wirtschaft & Ausfuhrkontrolle
– Erneuerbare Energien –
Frankfurter Straße 29–35
65760 Eschborn
Germany
Tel.: +49 6196 908-625
Fax: +49 6196 908-800
www.bafa.de/1/en/bafa/tasks.htm

Umweltbank
Applications:
Umweltbank AG
Laufertorgraben 6
90489 Nürnberg
Germany
Tel.: +49 911 5308-123
Fax: +49 911 5308-129
E-Mail: service@umweltbank.de
Internet: www.umweltbank.de

References

Deutsche Energie-Agentur GmbH (ed.):
Bauen für die Zukunft;
Möller Druck und Verlag, Berlin, 2004

Deutsche Energie-Agentur GmbH (ed.):
Modernisierungsratgeber Energie;
Konradin Druck GmbH, Berlin, 2003

European Renewable Energy Council (ed.):
Renewable Energy in Europe
Earthscan, London 2004

Gabriel, Ingo; Ladener, Heinz (ed.):
Vom Altbau zum Niedrigenergiehaus;
Ökobuch Verlag, Staufen, 2004

Gänßmantel, Jürgen; Geburtig, Gerd;
Eßman, Frank:
EnEV und Bauen im Bestand – Energie-
effiziente Gebäudeinstandsetzung;
Verlag Bauwesen, Berlin, 2006

Glücklich, Detlef (ed.):
Ökologisches Bauen
DVA, Munich, 2005

Gonzalo, Roberto; Habermann, Karl:
Energy Efficient Architecture
Birkhäuser, Basel 2006

Guy, Simon; Farmer, Graham
Reinterpreting Sustainable Architecture
Taylor and Francis, Oxford 2005

Halliday, Sandy:
Sustainable Construction
Elsevier, London 2006

Hastings, Robert; Wall, Maria (ed.):
Sustainable Solar Housing
Earthscan London

Hausladen, Gerhard et al.:
ClimaDesign
Callwey-Verlag, Munich, 2005

Hawthorne, Christopher; Alanna Stang:
The Green House
Princeton Architectural Press, NY
2005

Hyde, Richard (ed.):
Bioclimatic Housing
Earthscan, London 2007

Jester, Katharina; Schneider, Enno:
Weiterbauen. Konzepte, Projekte, Details;
Bauwerk Verlag, Berlin, 2002

Königstein, Thomas:
Ratgeber energiesparendes Bauen;
Fraunhofer IRB Verlag, Stuttgart, 2004,
2nd, revised edition

Kolb, Bernhard:
Nachhaltiges Bauen in der Praxis
Blok-Verlag, Munich, 2004

Krüger, Erich Prof. Dr.:
Konstruktiver Wärmeschutz
Niedrigenergie-Hochbaukonstruktion
Rudolf-Müller-Verlag, Cologne, 2000

Leutner, Bernd; Famira, Andrea M.;
Reimann, Volker: Bedarfsgerechte
Modernisierung von Wohnsiedlungen
der 1950er und 1960er Jahre;
Fraunhofer IRB Verlag, Stuttgart, 2006

National Calculation Methodology for
Determining the Energy Performance of
Buildings
NBS, Newcastle 2006

Pistohl, Wolfgang:
Handbuch der Gebäudetechnik
vol. 2 – Heizung/Lüftung/Energiesparen
Werner-Verlag, Neuwied, 2005, 5th edition

Roaf, Sue:
Closing the Loop
Benchmarks for Sustainable Buildings
NBS, Newcastle 2004

Sassi, Paola:
Strategies for Sustainable Architecture
Taylor and Francis, Oxford 2006

Schäden bei der energetischen
Modernisierung. 40. Bausachverstän-
digen-Tag 2005 proceedings;
Fraunhofer IRB Verlag, Stuttgart, 2005

Smith, Peter
Architecture in a Climate of Change
Elsevier, London 2005

Szokolay, Steven:
The Basis of Sustainable Design
Princeton Architectural Press, NY 2004

Techem AG:
Energie Kennwerte. Hilfen für den Woh-
nungswirt, Eine Studie der Techem AG;
Public Relations GmbH, Eschborn, 2005

Voss, Karsten et al.:
Bürogebäude mit Zukunft
TÜV-Verlag, Cologne

Zürcher, Christoph; Frank, Thomas:
Bauphysik, Bau und Energie vol. 2
vdf Hochschulverlag AG an der
ETH Zürich, 2004, 2nd, revised edition

Internet sources

www.e-impact.org
International project to promote the intro-
    duction of energy certificates
www.epbd-ca.org
EU project for the rational implementation
    of the EPBD
www.buildingsplatform.org
Informationsplattform zur EPBD
www.sustenergy.org
Information platform for the Sustainable
    Energy Europe Campaign 2005-2008
www.eplabel.org
International project with instructions for
    the compilation of energy certificates
    for non-residential buildings
www.eebd.org
Information platform for the start of the
    Electronic Energy Buildings Directive,
    with training tools
www.europeanpassivehouses.org
Information on passive-energy buildings
www.iso.org
Homepage of the International Organisa-
    tion for Standardisation
www.rehva.com
Homepage of the largest HVAC associa-
    tion in Europe
www.annex36.com/
    An international project that analyses
    energy-optimised refurbishment
    measures for existing educational esta-
    blishments.www.bine.info/
    Informationsdienst zu erneuerbarer Ener-
    gie und neuen Energiespartechniken
www.dena.de/en/
    The website of the German Energy
    Agency (DEnA).
www.energy-server.com/
    A platform for renewable energies and
    energy-efficient building and refurbish-
    ment.
www.iwu.de/homep_e.htm
    The website of the Institute for Housing
    & Development, a research institution of
    the federal state of Hesse and the city
    of Darmstadt.

www.solarbau.de/english_version/index.htm
    A website devoted to solar energy-
    optimised building.
www.umweltbundesamt.de/index-e.htm
    The website of the Federal Environment
    Agency includes comprehensive data
    on CO_2 emissions.
www.oeko.de/service/gemis/en/index.htm
    Information on the determination and
    evaluation of pollution emissions.
www.passiv.de/
    The homepage of the Passive House
    Institute.
www.ise.fraunhofer.com/
    The homepage of the Fraunhofer
    Institute for Solar Energy Systems

Index

Picture credits

The authors and publishers would like to express their sincere gratitude to all those who have assisted in the production of this book, be it through providing photos or artwork or granting permission to reproduce their documents or providing other information. All the drawings in this book were specially commissioned. Photographs not specifically credited were taken by the architects or are works photographs or were supplied from the archives of the magazine DETAIL. Despite intensive endeavours we were unable to establish copyright ownership in just a few cases; however, copyright is assured. Please notify us accordingly in such instances.

page 6, 54, 106:
Christian Schittich, Munich

page 12:
Beat Glanzmann/zefa/corbis

page 22:
Frank Kaltenbach, Munich

page 74, 82 top, 83:
Heinrich Helfenstein, Zürich

page 76 top:
PP-Engineering, Riehen

page 76 bottom:
Fritz Haller Bauen und Forschen GmbH, Solothurn

page 78:
Reynaers AG, Frauenfeld

page 81:
Walter Mair, Zürich

page 86 top, 87:
Wolf-Dieter Gericke, Waiblingen

page 88:
Siegfried Wameser, Munich

page 94 top:
Jean-Luc Valentin, Frankfurt am Main

page 96:
Archiv Olgiati, Flims

Full-page plates

page 6:
The Sun, source of solar energy

page 12:
Igloo at night

page 22:
Münchener Rückversicherungs-
Gesellschaft, Munich
Baumschlager & Eberle, Vaduz

page 54:
Lehrter railway station, Berlin
von Gerkan Marg & Partner, Hamburg

page 74:
Office building, Zürich
Romero & Schäfle, Zürich

page 96:
Arts centre, Flims
Valerio Olgiati, Flims

page 106:
Granite roof covering, Corippo, Ticino